180 Doodle Quilting Designs

FREE-MOTION IDEAS for BLOCKS, BORDERS, and BEYOND

COMPILED BY **Karen M. Burns**

Martingale®
Create with Confidence

180 Doodle Quilting Designs:
Free-Motion Ideas for Blocks, Borders, and Beyond
© 2016 by Martingale & Company®

Martingale®
19021 120th Ave. NE, Ste. 102
Bothell, WA 98011-9511 USA
ShopMartingale.com

Printed in China
21 20 19 18   8 7 6 5 4 3

Library of Congress Cataloging-in-Publication Data
is available upon request.

ISBN: 978-1-60468-799-6

MISSION STATEMENT

We empower makers who use fabric and yarn to make life more enjoyable.

CREDITS

PUBLISHER AND
CHIEF VISIONARY OFFICER
Jennifer Erbe Keltner

CONTENT DIRECTOR
Karen Costello Soltys

DESIGN MANAGER
Adrienne Smitke

MANAGING EDITOR
Tina Cook

PRODUCTION MANAGER
Regina Girard

ACQUISITIONS EDITOR
Karen M. Burns

PHOTOGRAPHER
Brent Kane

TECHNICAL EDITOR
Beth Bradley

ILLUSTRATORS
Christine Erikson
Anne Moscicki
Rose Wright

COPY EDITOR
Durby Peterson

Contents

Introduction

Think back to first grade for a moment. Do you remember picking up your markers or crayons and doodling to your heart's content? Do you remember being worried about whether your drawings turned out perfectly? Of course not! That's because the act of drawing is purely fun. But it seems that the older we get, the more we get stuck on the idea that doodling or sketching is an activity reserved for artists. The truth is that doodling doesn't require a Fine Arts degree; it's simply a pleasant and relaxing way for anyone to put their thoughts on paper.

As quilters, many of us have the same roadblocks when it comes to finishing our quilts. We worry about choosing the perfect quilting design, and then quilting it absolutely flawlessly. These worries can be paralyzing, often resulting in a closetful of abandoned quilt tops. With 180 amazing and unique designs to choose from, this book aims to help you get past those barriers and recapture some of that magical first-grade enthusiasm. Not only does doodling make your quilting ideas tangible, it also helps your creative process by calming and focusing your mind. Another invaluable benefit of doodling is the muscle memory that comes from lots of practice. When you're ready to quilt the design, you'll feel comfortable and confident, and your quilting skills will grow along with your enjoyment of the process.

Before long, that stack of unfinished quilt tops will start to disappear, and you'll remember why you love this hobby of quilting in the first place. Just like drawing with markers and crayons, quilting is purely fun.

Happy doodling!

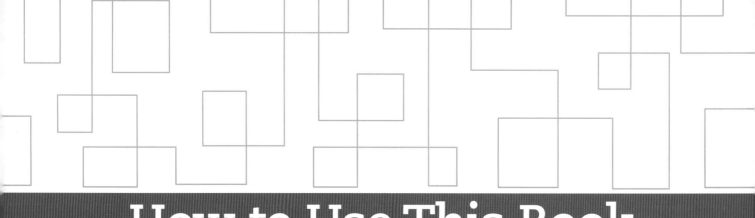

How to Use This Book

Not only will you find an inspiring and diverse assortment of quilting designs in this book, you'll also discover a great resource for developing your free-motion quilting skills, whether you quilt on a long-arm or a home sewing machine. Each design set includes three coordinating designs (a square block, a border, and a setting triangle) to give your quilt a cohesive look. The sets are divided into four categories so you can easily select a design that suits your skills as well as the style of your quilt.

The design sets include useful stitching tips from the designers, as well as arrows showing where to start and end your stitching. Some designs in the book are color coded with black and blue lines. These two colors are meant show separate elements of the design that have different stopping and starting points. You might stitch an outline shape first (black lines), and then fill in the shape or negative space with swirls or other motifs (blue lines).

Trace the Doodles

Once a set of designs catches your eye, it's time to tap into the power of doodling. While you might be tempted to jump right to stitching, doodling on paper is an invaluable step that allows you to get accustomed to the rhythm of the design and create the muscle memory you need to stitch in a continous line. It also gives you a chance to practice without the pressure of using thread and fabric.

You'll need a few easy-to-find drawing supplies to embark on your doodling adventure. Invest in a simple sketchbook with unlined pages, as well as felt-tip pens or markers. Test out a few types of pens to find one that has a smooth feel and flow for sketching. It's also useful to have a pad of tracing paper to practice doodling directly over the designs in the book. This will help you understand the easiest stitching path to take as you follow the arrows.

Start by placing tracing paper over the design. Place your pen at the "start" dot, and then slowly trace the line following the arrows, doing your best to keep a continuous line and not lift your pen. As you trace, you'll start to understand how the design is formed, and you'll get a feel for the repetitive motion that you'll be using. Repeat this process as many times as you like, building up confidence that you can doodle the design without needing to trace it.

Doodle Freehand

Next, try doodling the design freehand in your sketchbook. Using the original design as a reference, doodle the design on paper while maintaining a continuous line. Don't worry about drawing perfectly or making a pretty picture. The process of doodling is all about developing your muscle memory and finding a tempo that feels natural and relaxed to you.

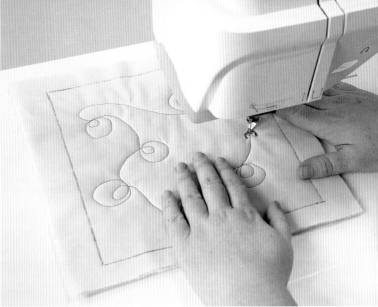

Left: Doodle the design freehand, using the original for reference.
Right: Practice quilting on a sample quilt sandwich.

The goal is to feel calm and confident when it's time to stitch. Remember that it's okay if your doodles aren't an exact match to the original drawing. You'll find that the more you practice, the better your doodles will be.

Now that you're well acquainted with the rhythm of the design, it's time to graduate from pen and paper to needle and thread. Make a few small practice quilt sandwiches from fabric and batting. Use a thread color that doesn't contrast too highly with the fabric; otherwise, you might find yourself fixating on mistakes. Draw the outline of the quilting shape on the fabric to use as a framework. Relax your mind and body, lower the needle, and start stitching. Aim for a stitching speed that feels efficient without being rushed. Allow the muscle memory that you developed through doodling to guide your movement. The process is much more important than the final product, so don't focus on making a beautiful quilt sandwich. When you've filled one quilt sandwich with doodles, start stiching on another one. Once again, practice is key. Even practicing for 10 to 15 minutes at a time will build your skills and confidence and you'll quickly see improvement.

Practice Stitching

Many designs contain motifs that can be stitched in different ways, so practicing will help you find a method you like best. For example, when stitching pebbles, it's possible to create them by retracing your previous circles or by stitching them in a figure-eight pattern. Or you can stitch half-circles in one direction and complete the circles in the opposite direction.

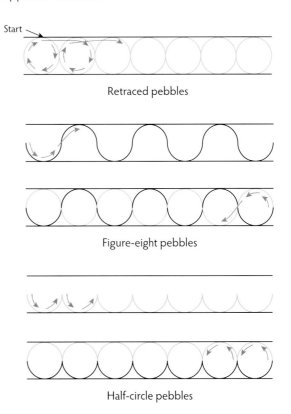

Play with the scale, size, density, and combination of design elements to customize them for your projects. Don't be surprised if you start to dream up doodle designs of your own, so always keep that sketchbook handy!

Double Wavy Lines

DESIGNED BY VICKI RUEBEL

Double wavy lines are the best-kept secret in the quilting world. Perfect for beginning quilters, this super simple design adds great texture to a quilt. The use of a double wavy line in a border creates a wavy piano-key look that's simple to execute with no marking. And you don't have to worry about retracing the previous stitching perfectly! What could be easier?

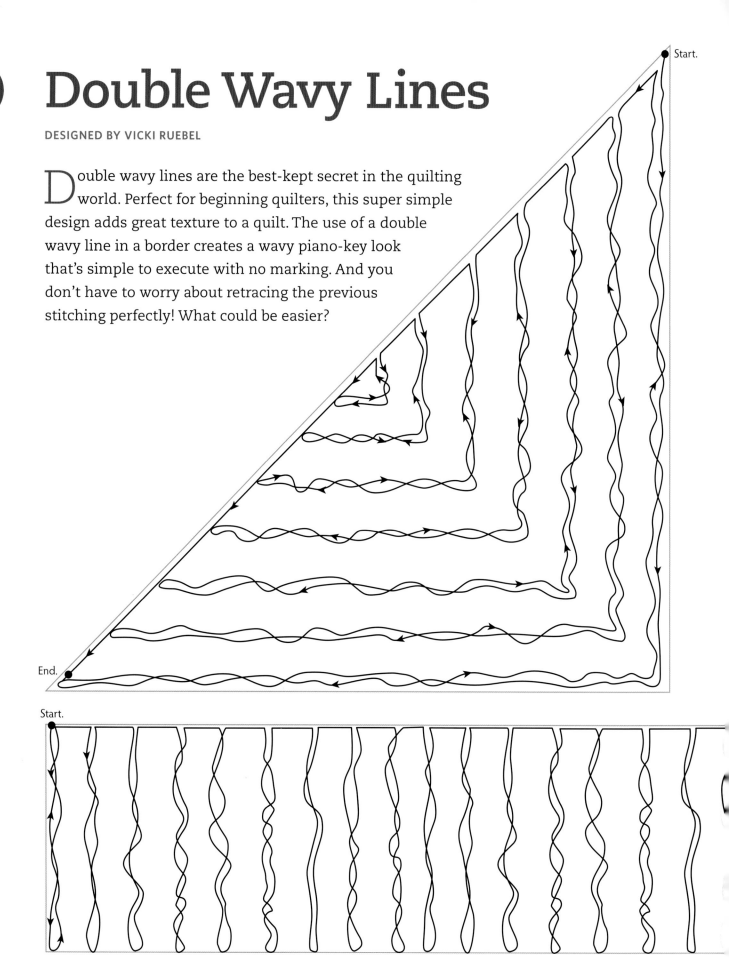

Start.

End.

Start.

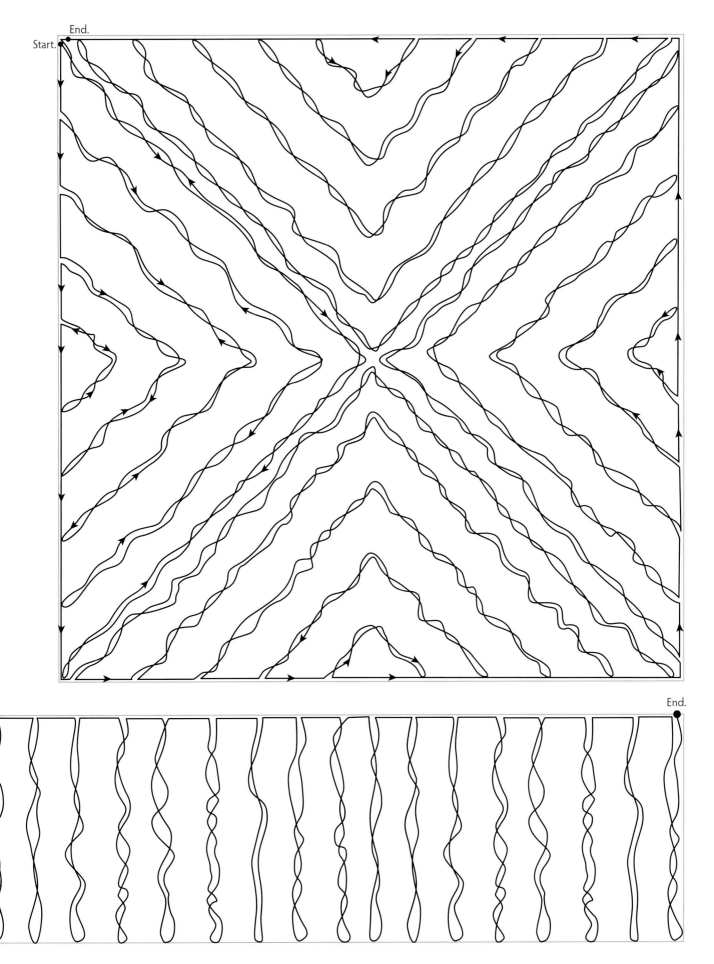

End.

Start.

End.

Squiggles and Giggles

DESIGNED BY VICKI RUEBEL

Alternating dense quilting with more loosely spaced quilting adds lots of texture and definition to a quilt. The tight and wavy lines complement each other and create interesting variation. Plus, it's easy to customize the design to fit any shape. This simple yet effective technique is a great option for beginners and seasoned quilters alike.

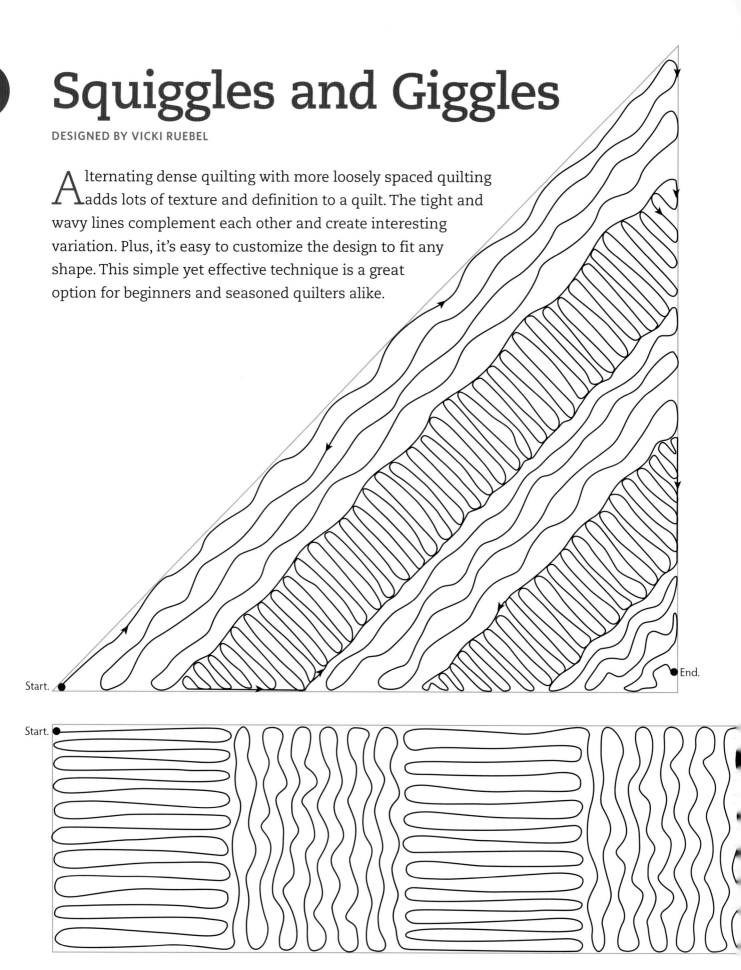

Start.

Start.

End.

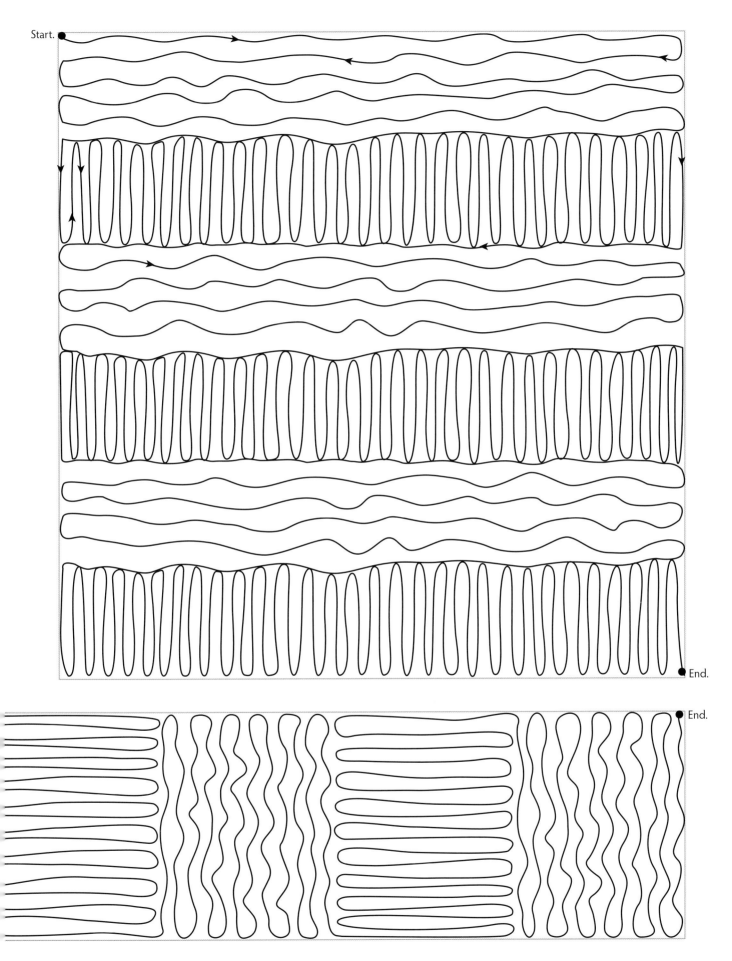

Wavy Crosshatch

DESIGNED BY VICKI RUEBEL

Wavy Crosshatch is a fun and easy design that quickly generates texture. The wavy lines don't need to be marked, as the imperfection adds to the organic look. The scale of the crosshatching is easy to modify, allowing you to fit this design into both small and large areas, including narrow borders. First stitch the lines in one direction, and then stitch the perpendicular lines to complete the grid.

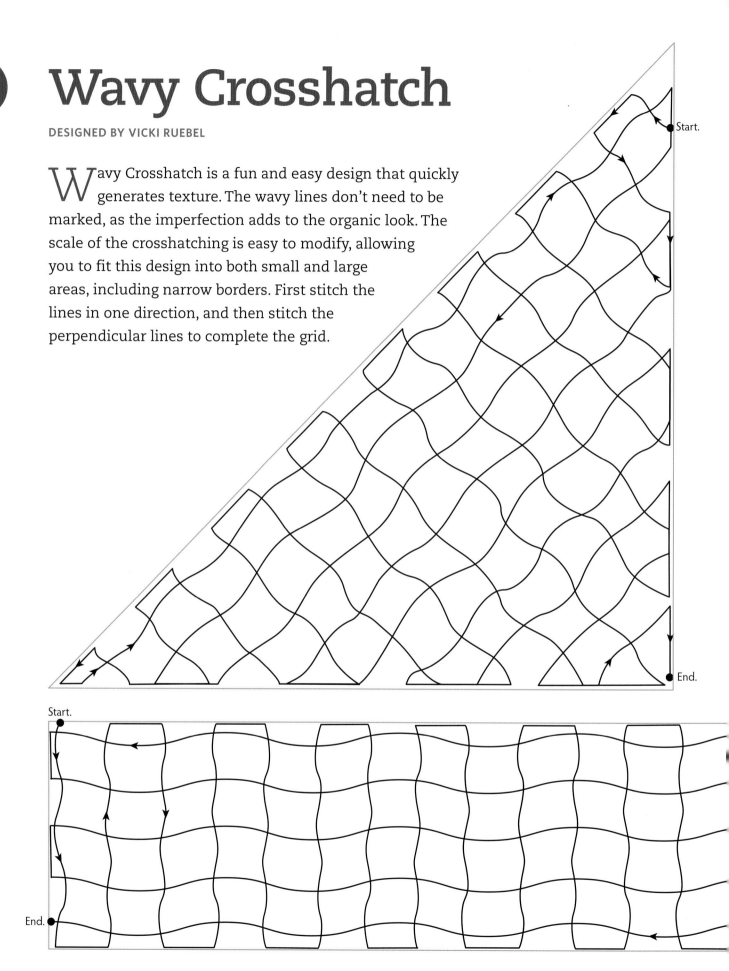

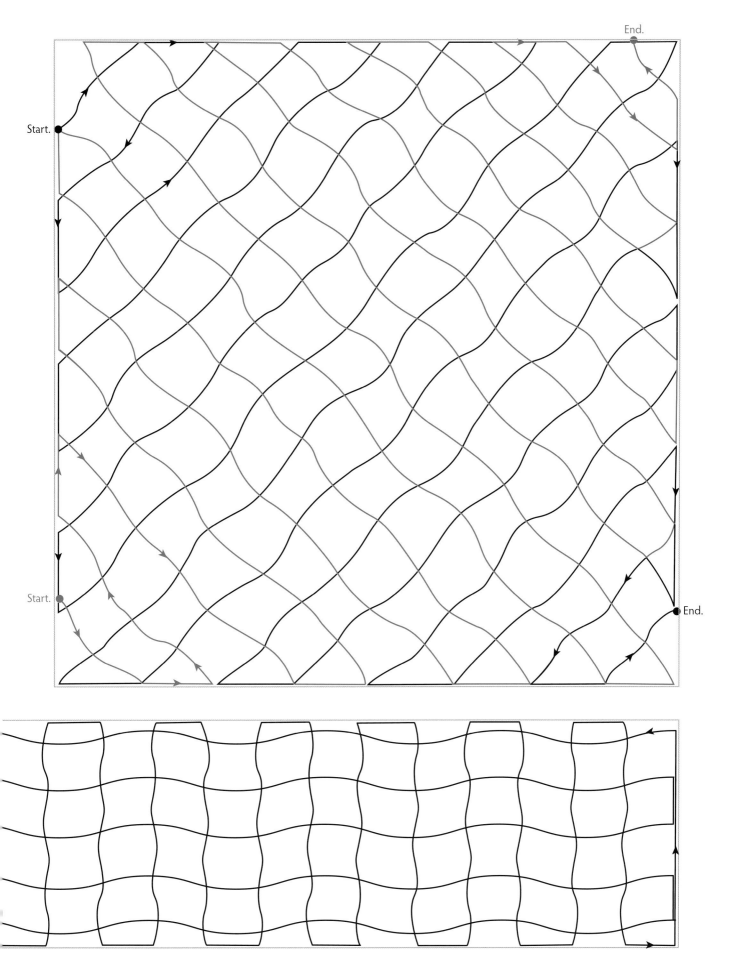

Start.

Start.

End.

End.

Daring Diamonds

DESIGNED BY VICKI RUEBEL

Create areas of dimension in your quilt by mixing unquilted diamonds (or squares) with tight lines. The diamonds aren't marked and are completely organic. This design works especially well in borders, but it can be modified to fit any shape. On the block and border, stitch outlines of the diamonds first, and then fill in the back-and-forth curved lines. On the triangle, stitch the upper and middle diamonds, the black curved lines, and then the last diamond. Fill in the remaining area with the curved lines shown in blue.

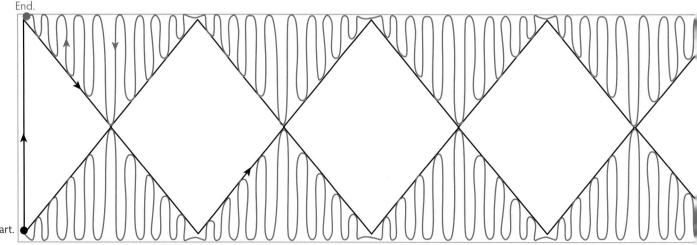

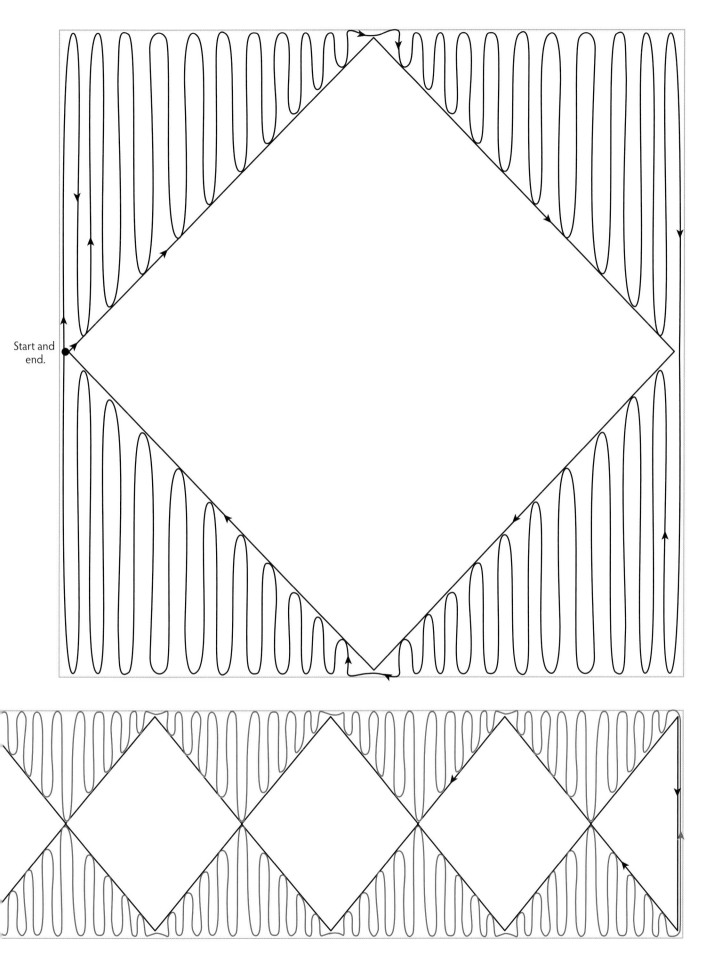

Start and end.

Zigzags

DESIGNED BY CHRISTA WATSON

Zigzags work well for modern quilts or any project with strong geometric shapes. The same basic zigzag shape can be scaled to fit any size or area. Mark the spacing of your lines before quilting if you want them to be even and symmetrical. For a more organic look, don't mark the lines and quilt the zigzags at random intervals instead. Practice drawing zigzags on a sketch pad first to get a feel for how the design is formed.

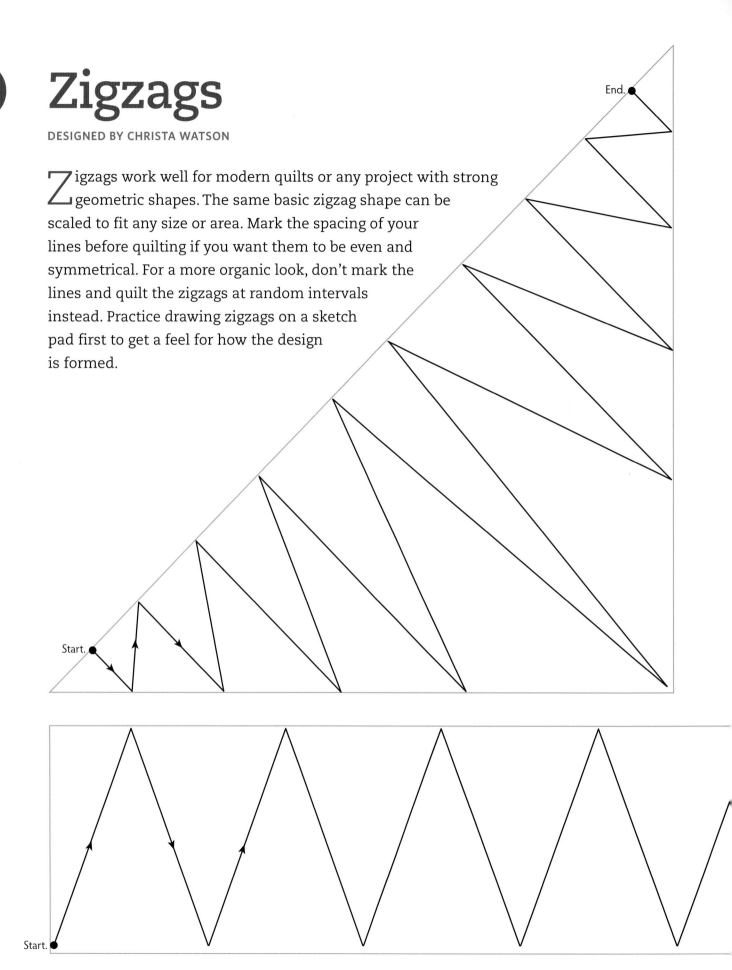

End.

Start.

Start.

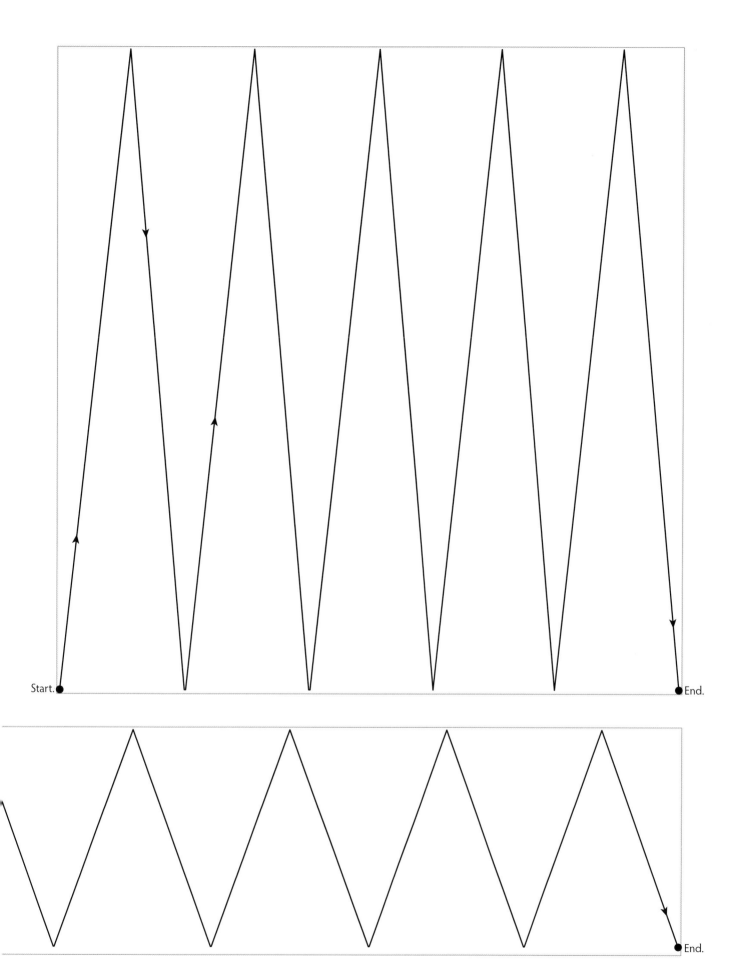

Start.

End.

End.

Arrowhead

DESIGNED BY APRIL ROSENTHAL

Triple triangles make for a striking and unique design element. Consider quilting two rows that interlock for an ornate chevron look, or align all the triangles in the same direction to create the look of prairie points. Quilting accurate diagonal lines can be tricky, especially on a long-arm machine. If you're having a hard time keeping them straight and tidy, use a ruler or marked line as a guide.

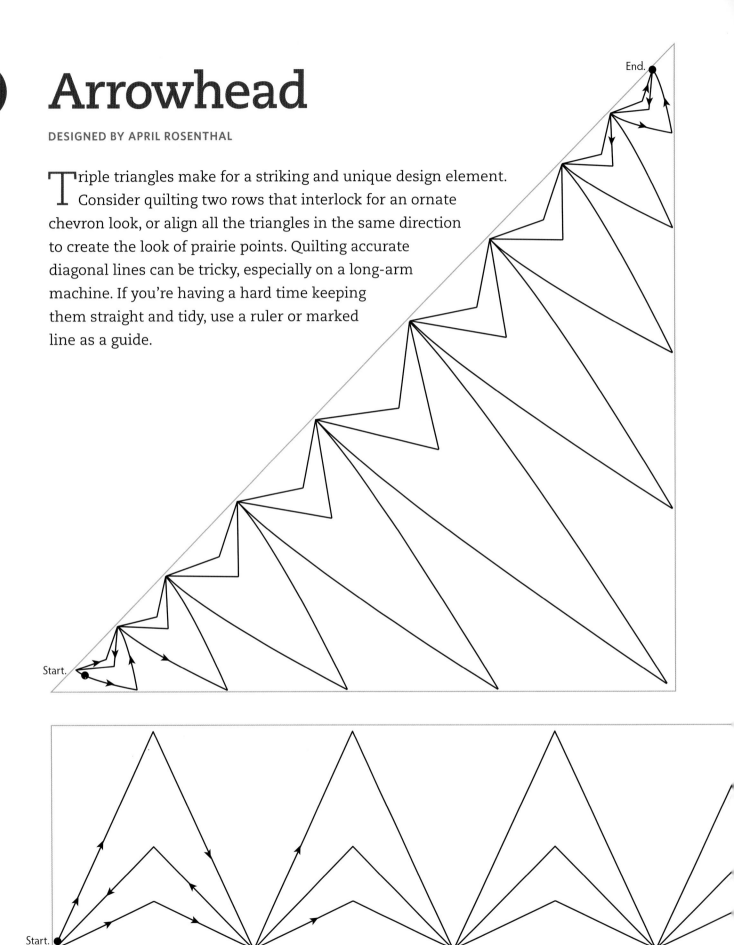

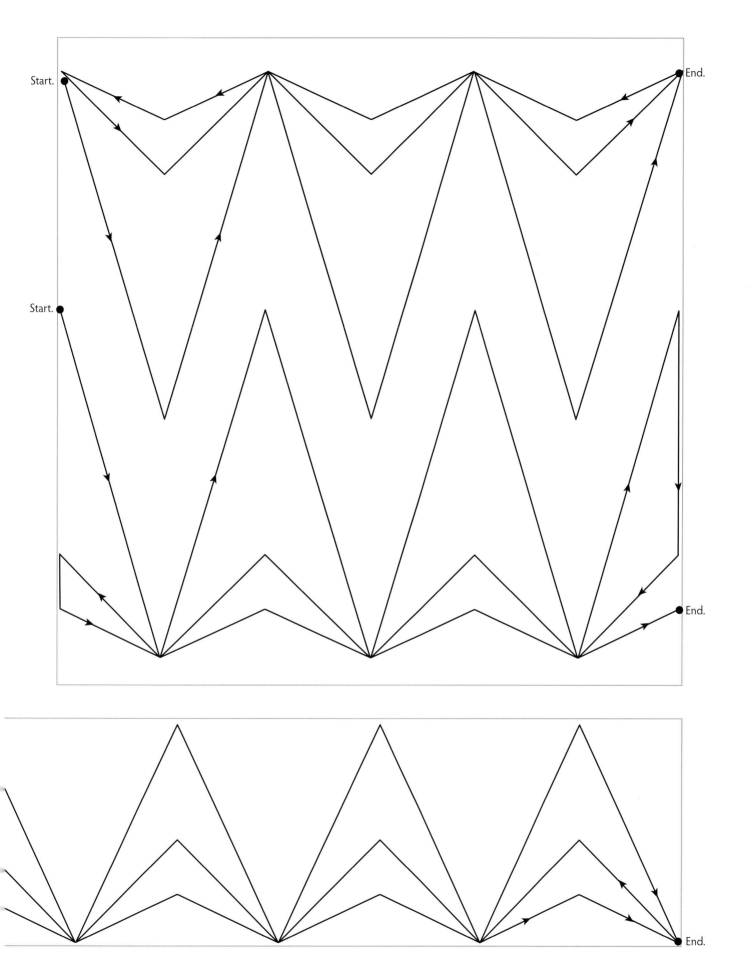

Cornered

DESIGNED BY APRIL ROSENTHAL

An angular take on the classic stipple, Cornered is a great option for beginning quilters because you don't have to worry about rules like not crossing over previous stitching lines! That makes it easy to fill all the spaces and return to spots you may have missed. Try using this design on a quilt with curves and enjoy the contrast. Or use it in a large scale as an allover design to add a modern slant to your finished quilt.

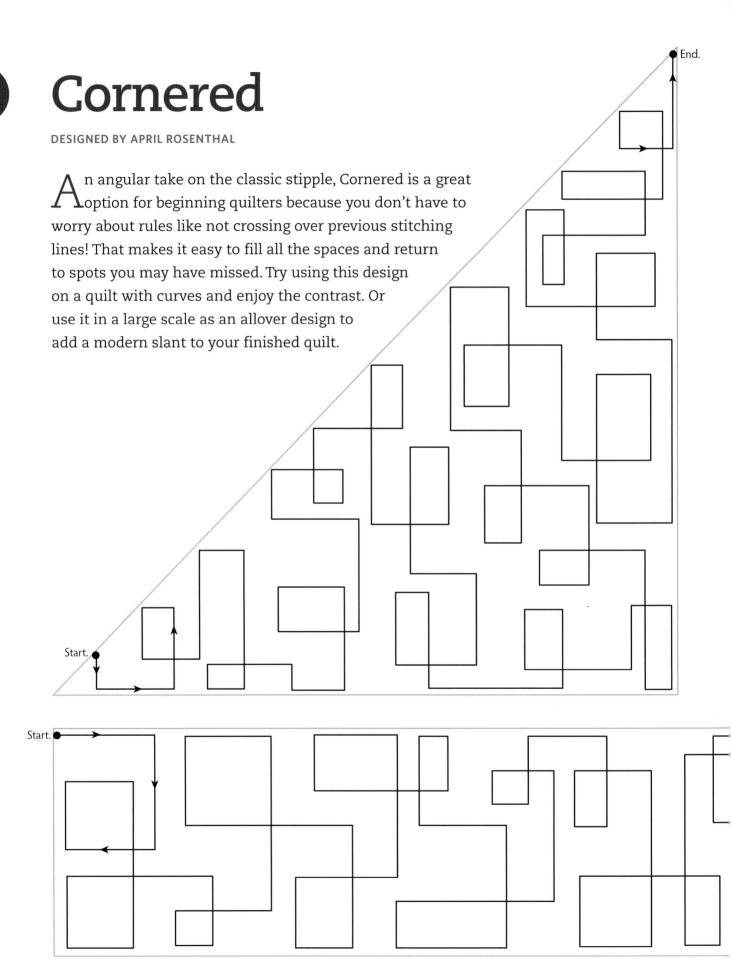

Start.

End.

End.

Square-Centric

DESIGNED BY APRIL ROSENTHAL

Fast and easy is the name of this game. Squares and rectangles make a graphic, modern design that easily fits into tight spaces and creates fabulous, channeled texture. As you work this design, you'll find it effortless to get into a rhythm and finish quickly. To keep the corners crisp and maximize the impact of this look, be sure to come to a complete stop before changing directions.

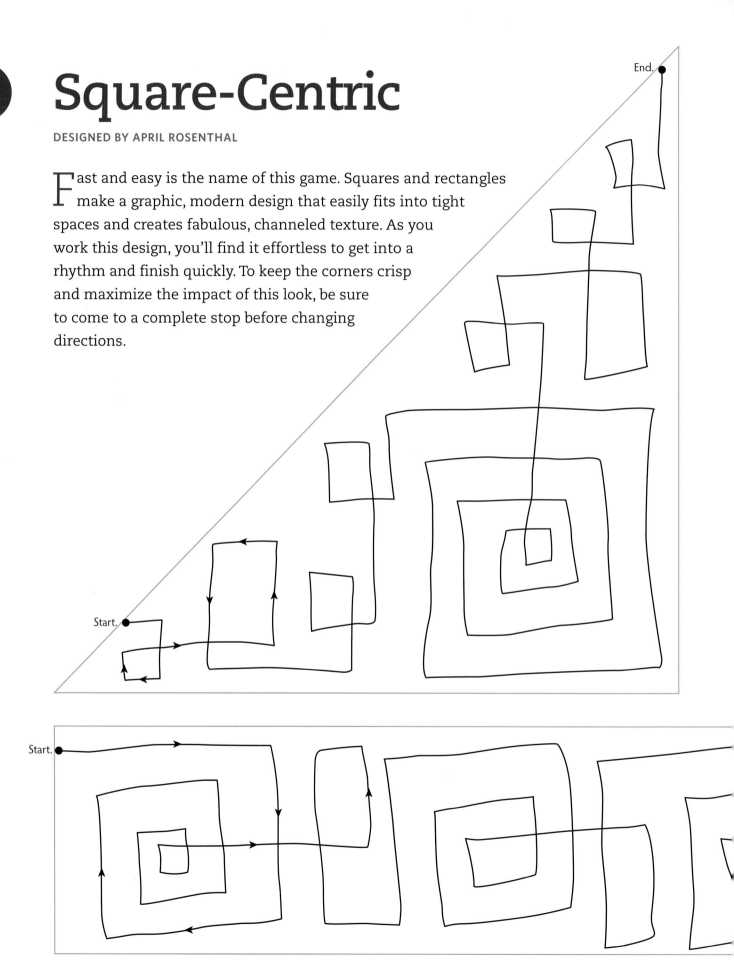

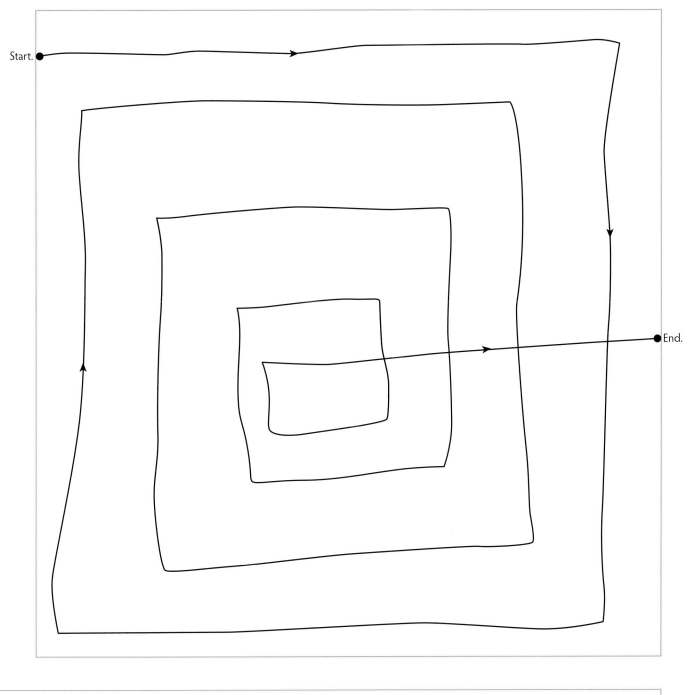

Start.

End.

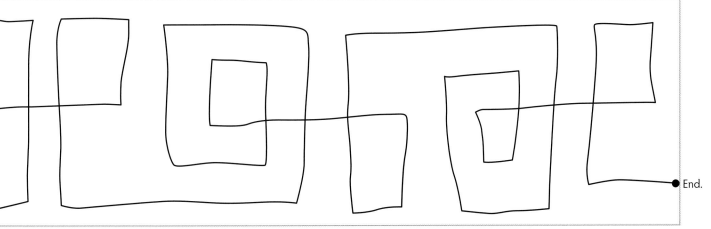

End.

Organic Checkerboard

DESIGNED BY MADDIE KERTAY

This design is all about the texture and relief of the threadwork, so use thread that's an exact color match or just slightly darker than the fabric. Start by creating the grid with a removable fabric marker (shown in blue), and then use your thread to fill alternate sections. The contrast between the stitched and unstitched areas makes this design an amazing fill. The checkerboard pattern is worked across two rows at a time before moving on to the next pair of rows.

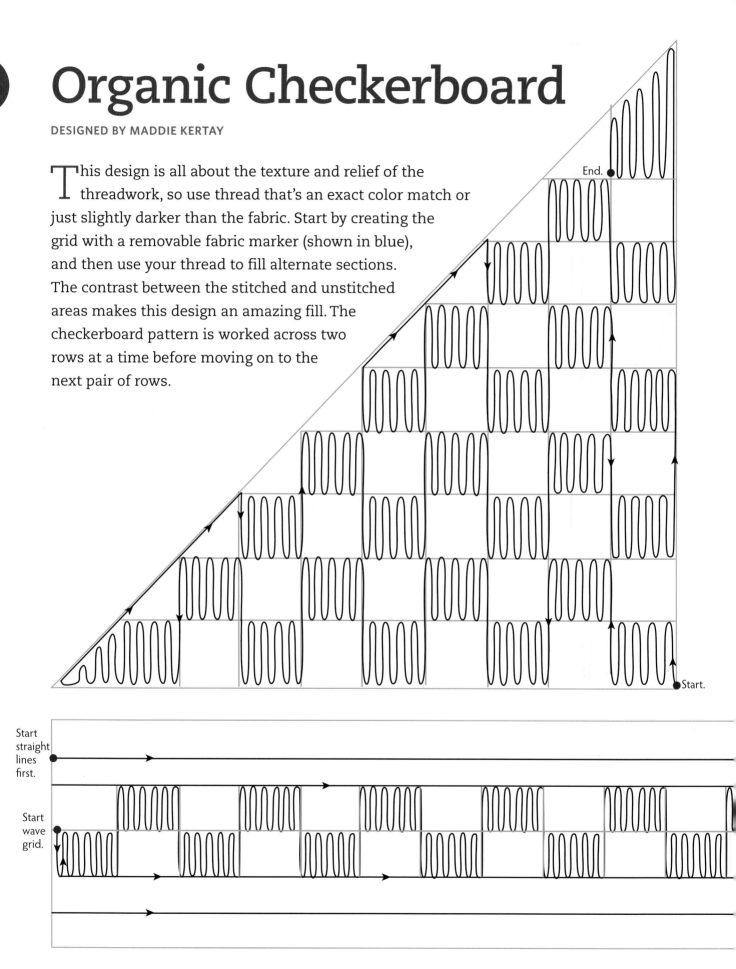

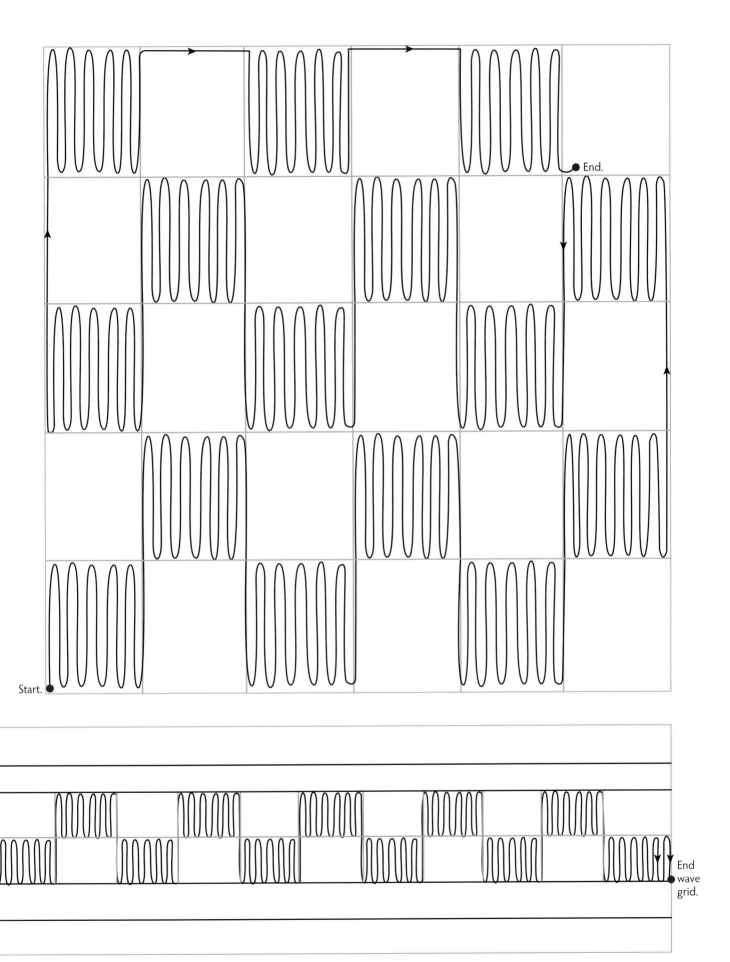

Start.

End.

End wave grid.

Lombard Street

DESIGNED BY APRIL ROSENTHAL

Re-create San Francisco's famous hairpin-turn street in quilting! Practice stitching back-and-forth lines in both vertical and horizontal directions so you can move between them easily. You'll get good at gauging how many lines you need to fill in a certain area and also at knowing when to change directions for the look you want.

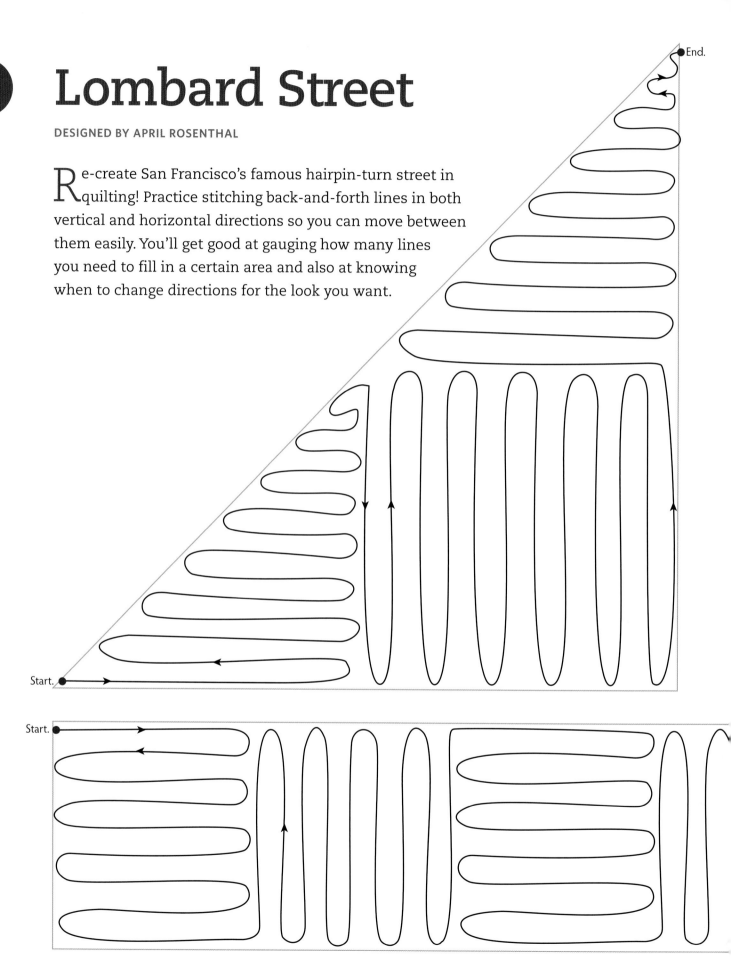

Start.

End.

End.

Waffle Weave

DESIGNED BY APRIL ROSENTHAL

Perpendicular lines make Waffle Weave a pattern that's easy to quilt, and the design creates texture so delicious you'll want to use it on every project. With practice, your lines will be evenly spaced and at right angles to one another. Start slowly and plan the lines so they fill the space evenly.

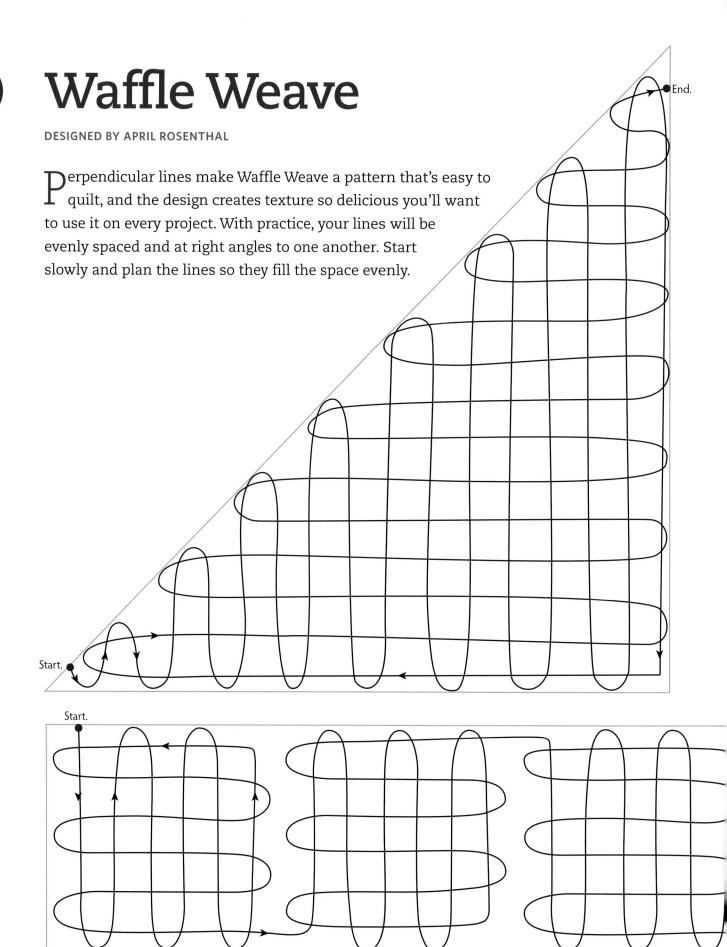

Start.

End.

Start.

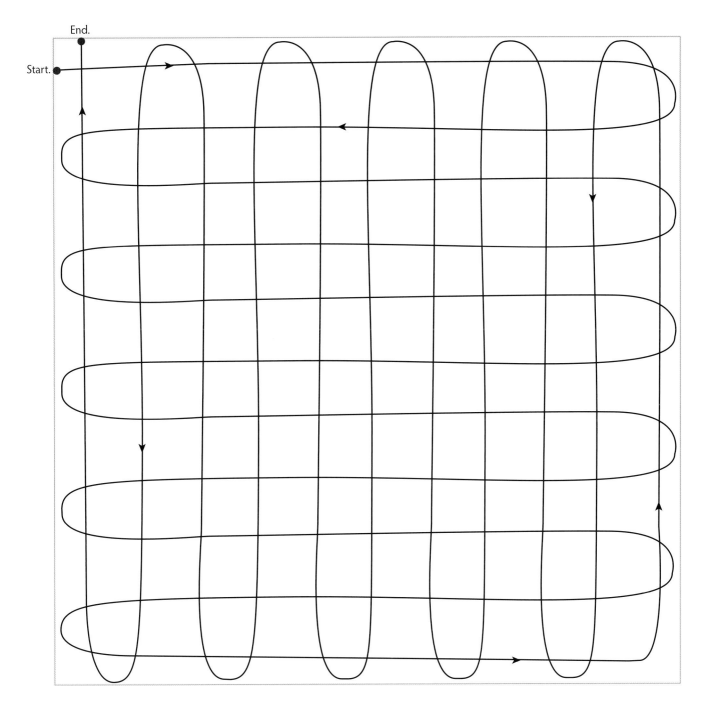

End.

Start.

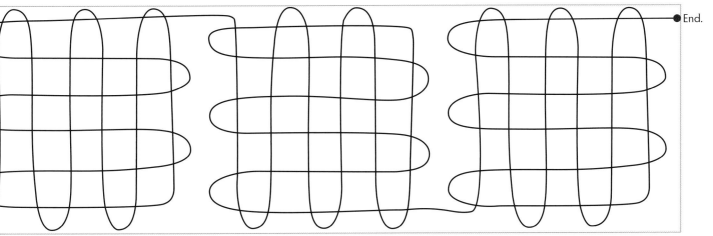

End.

Wavy Plaid

DESIGNED BY CHRISTA WATSON

The versatile Wavy Plaid looks great as a fill for any shape. To form the design in a block or border, start quilting on one side of the area and stitch a gently waving horizontal line to the other side. Stitch about ¼" from the line, and then quilt a parallel wavy line in the opposite direction. When you've filled in all the horizontal space, quilt vertical wavy lines in the same manner. When quilting a triangle shape, quilt the vertical lines first.

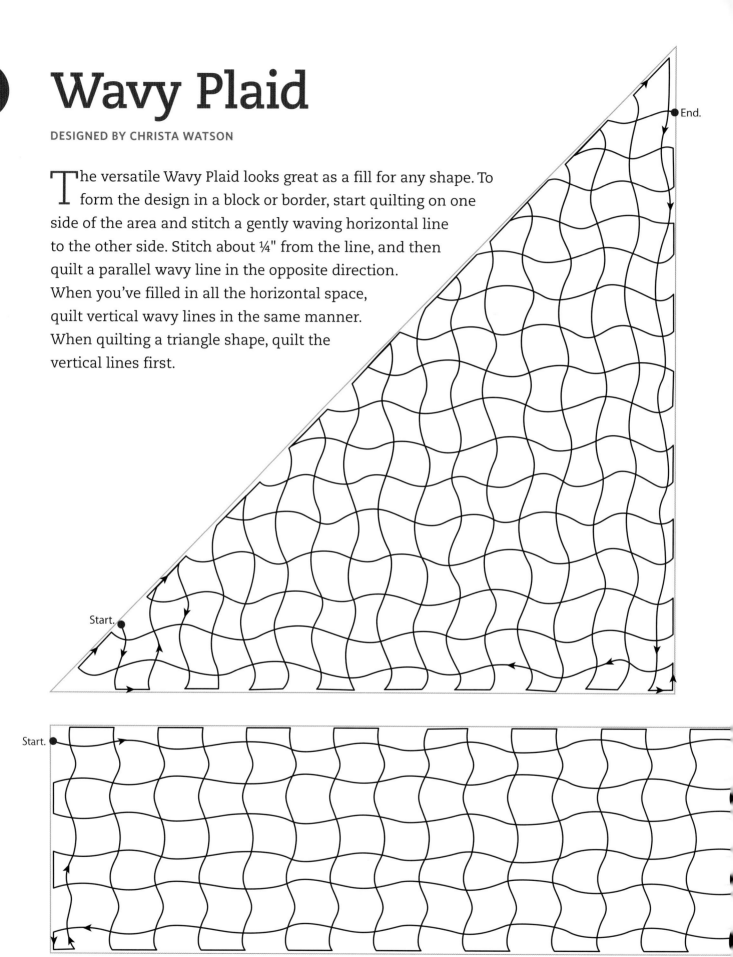

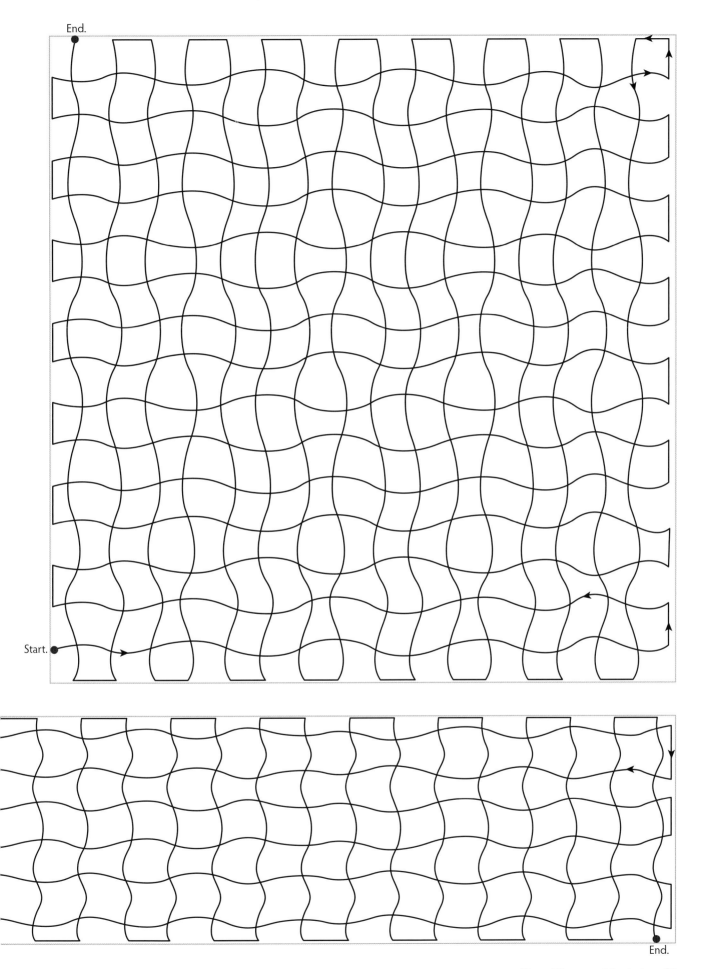

End.

Start.

End.

Jelly Bean

DESIGNED BY APRIL ROSENTHAL

Combining circular and oblong pebbles makes for a varied and interesting pattern that really shines in background spaces. You'll become quite good at retracing your stitches as you move around pebbles you've already sewn in order to reach areas you need to complete. To create denser quilting, simply make the pebbles smaller. For looser quilting, make the pebbles larger. To disguise areas where you have to retrace your stitches, choose a thread that blends nicely with the fabric color.

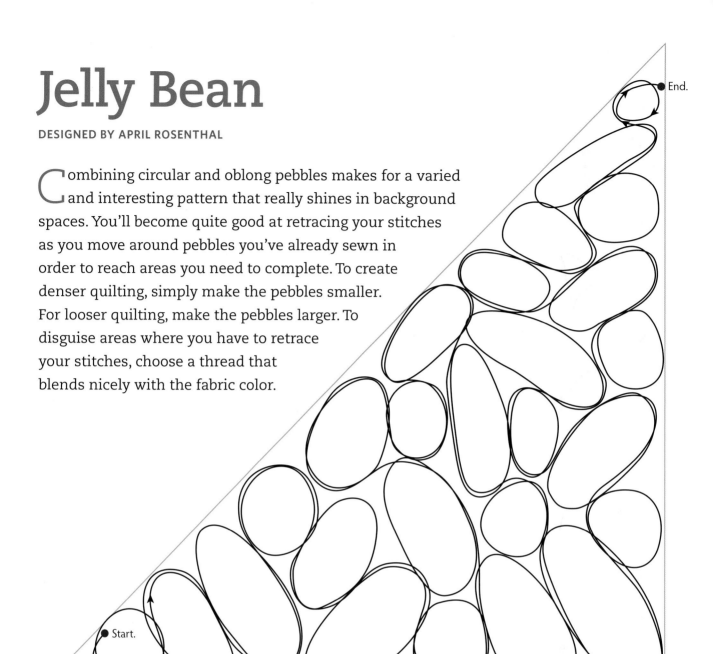

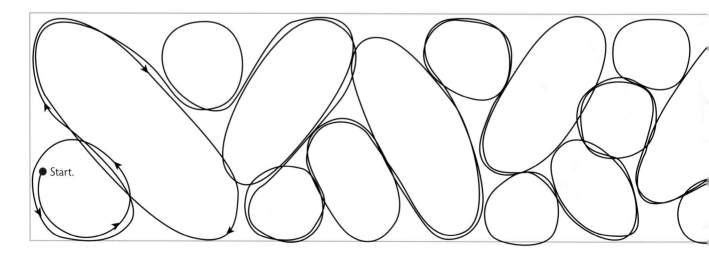

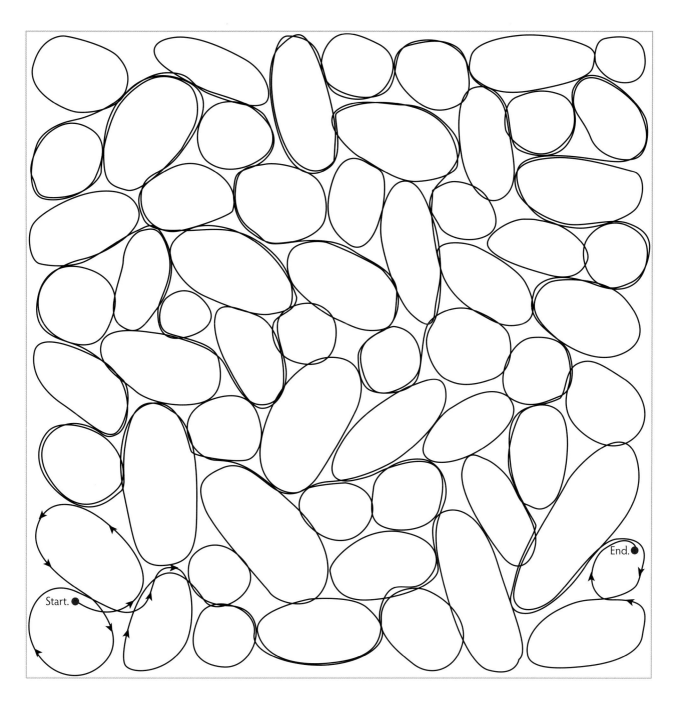

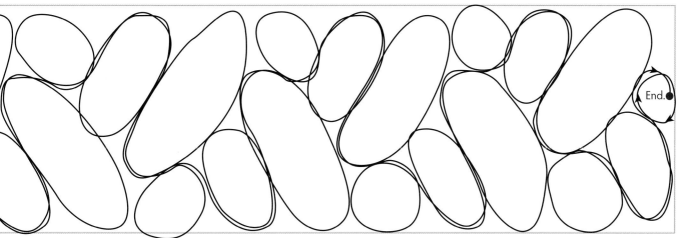

Pebble Garden

DESIGNED BY APRIL ROSENTHAL

Oval pebbles that are stacked or aligned in rows create lovely texture for an updated look that isn't too modern. Pebble Garden takes some practice so the ovals will touch without overlapping or being spaced too far apart, but the effort is worth it! This design can be quilted as densely or lightly as you like. Stitch the pebbles in a figure-eight style to avoid lots of retracing.

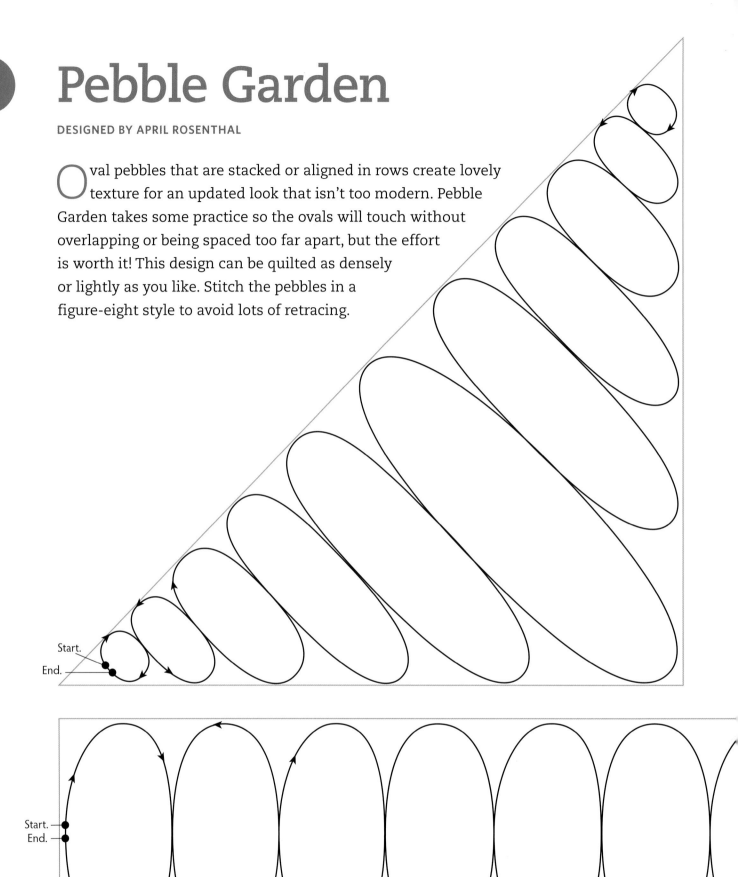

Start.

End.

Start.
End.

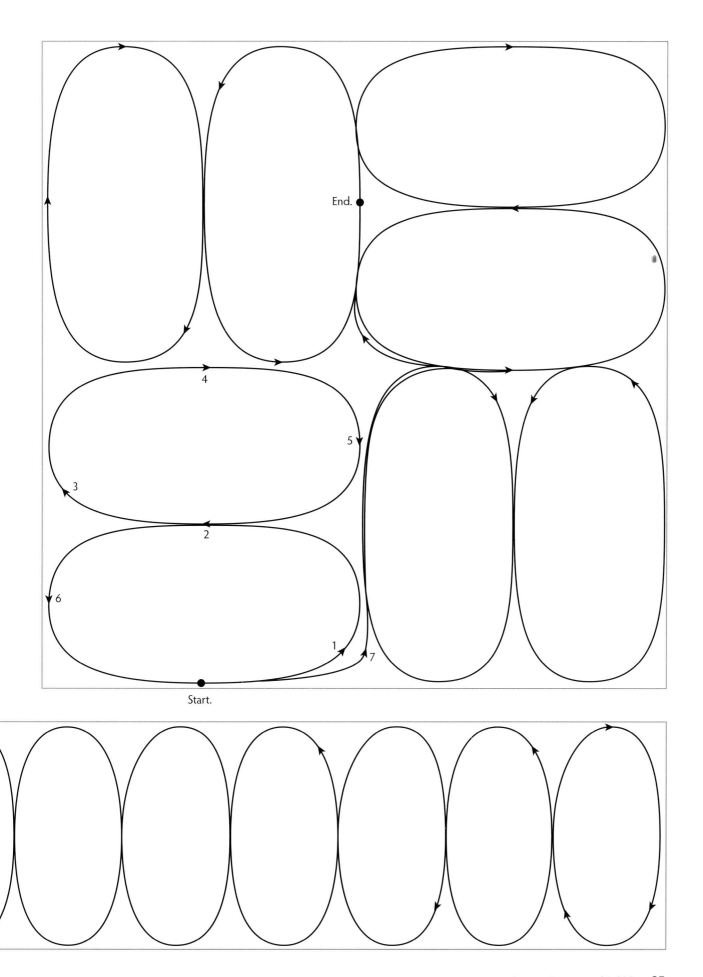

End.

Start.

4

5

3

2

6

1

7

Drip Drop

DESIGNED BY APRIL ROSENTHAL

Make raindrop shapes in different arrangements for a unique design that's adaptable to almost any space. The pointed end and curved lines make it easy to form quilted petals on a flower or a tip-to-tip border design. For the border, backtrack over one side of each shape in order to move to the next one. For the triangle, stitch the curved edges (shown in black), and then stitch the pointed ends (shown in blue). The block and setting-triangle designs can be stitched in one continuous line without the need for backtracking.

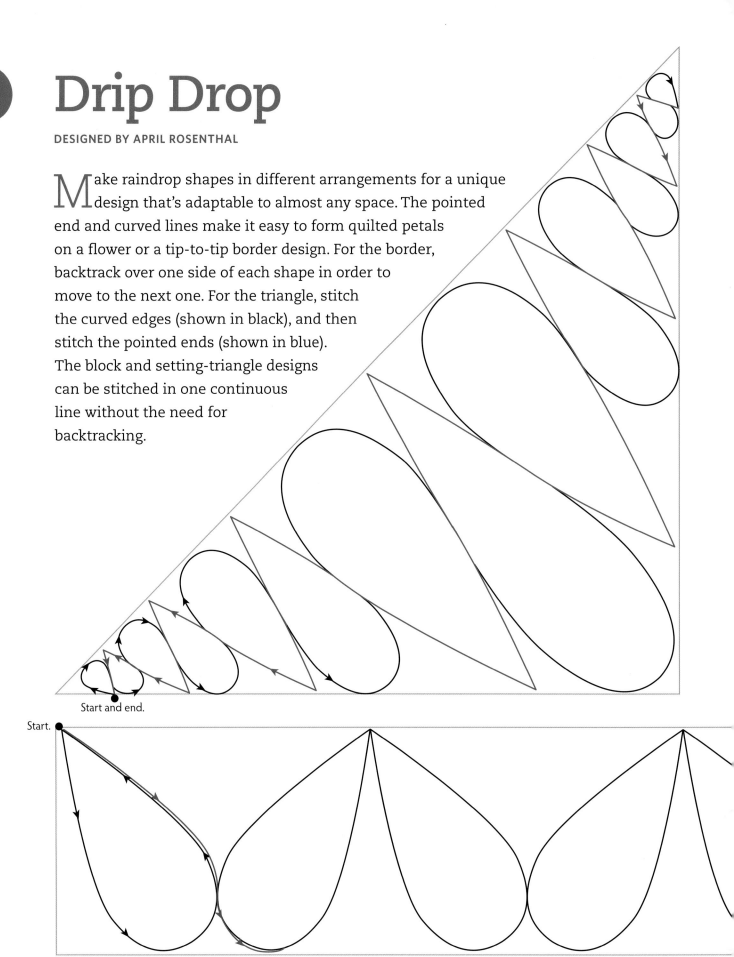

Start and end.

Start.

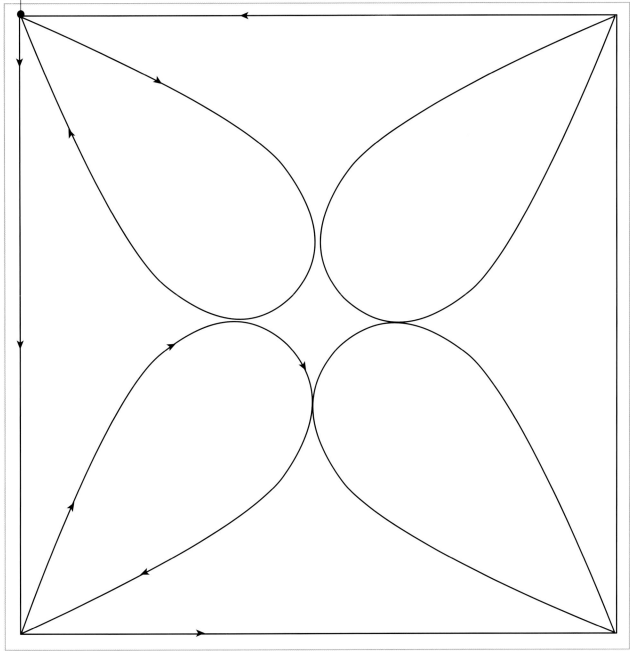

End.

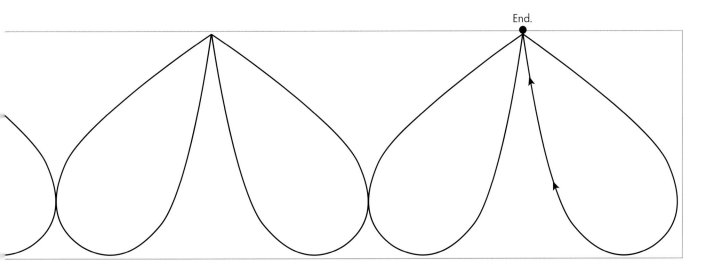

Rock and a Hard Place

DESIGNED BY APRIL ROSENTHAL

Play with contrast by using both straight lines and tiny pebbles. For a precise look, use the same number of vertical lines between each column of pebbles. If you prefer a more free-flowing approach, vary the number of vertical lines or vary the spacing. Move from pebble to pebble by retracing and reversing directions with each circle.

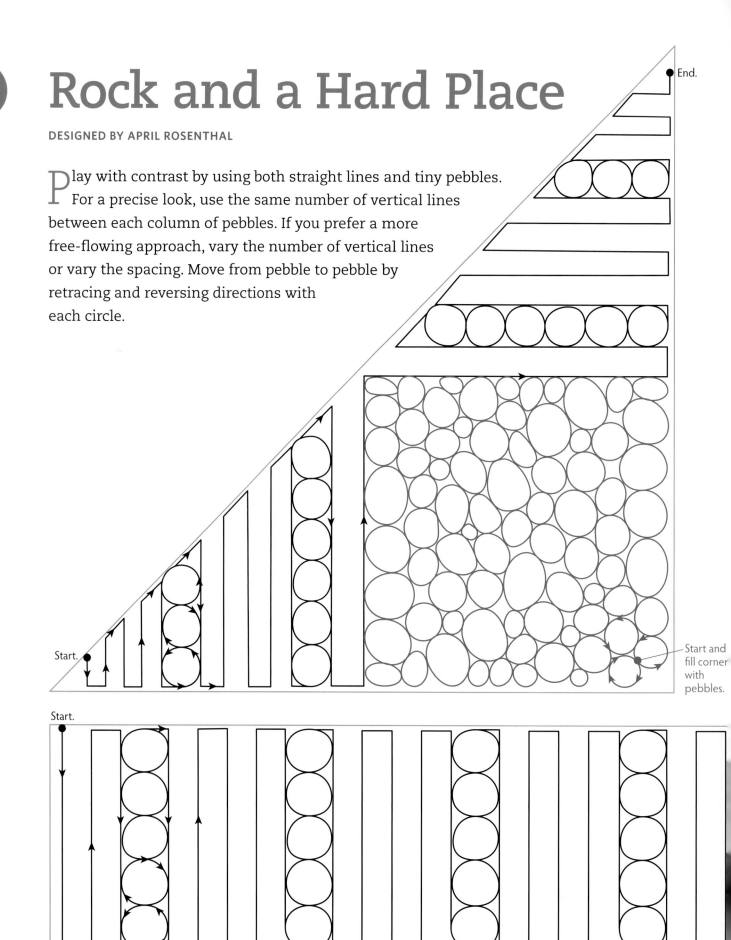

End.

Start.

Start and fill corner with pebbles.

Start.

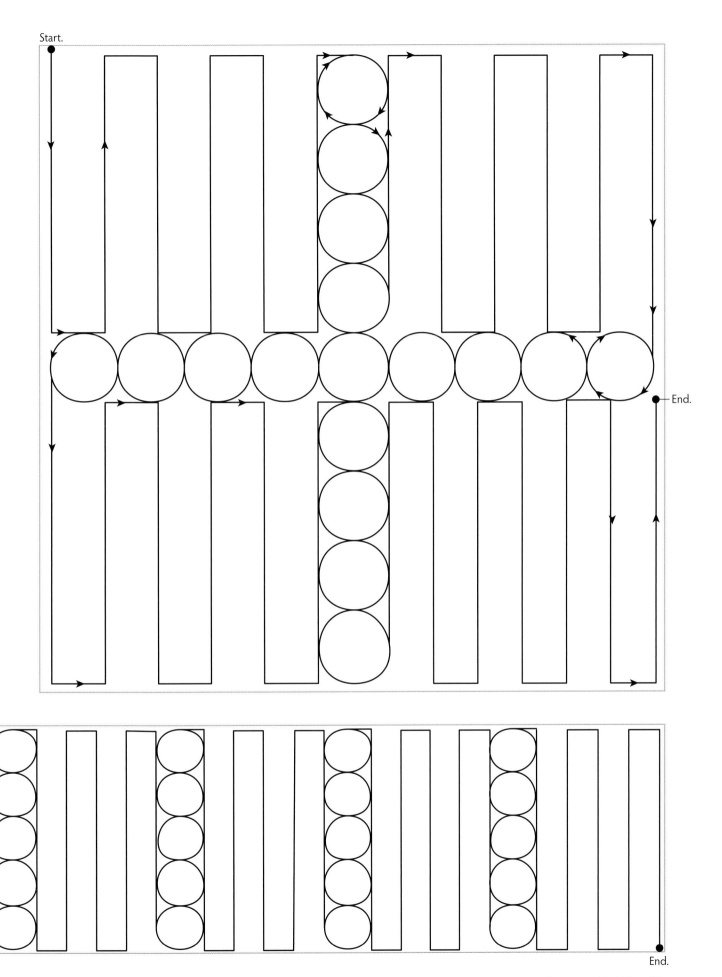

Start.

End.

Hills and Valleys

DESIGNED BY APRIL ROSENTHAL

To create a rickrack effect in your quilting, simply stitch a row of hills, and then an offset row of valleys. Practice using a smooth, fluid movement, stopping the machine at each change of direction to ensure a crisp point. This simple design can be worked both right to left and left to right on most long-arm machines without shredding the thread.

Start and end.

Start and end.

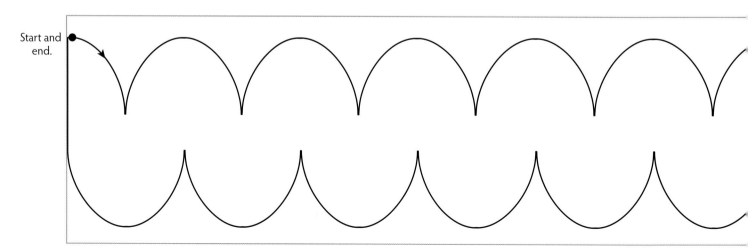

Start and end.

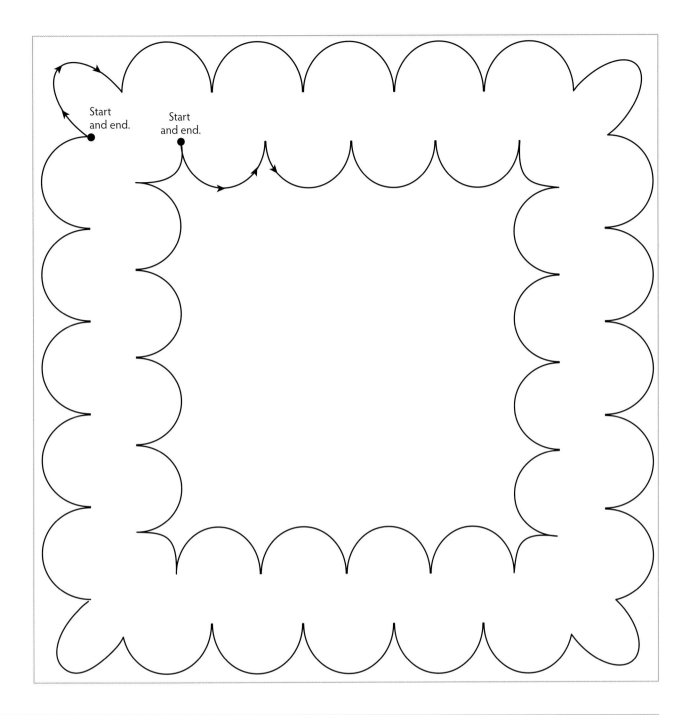

Start and end.

Start and end.

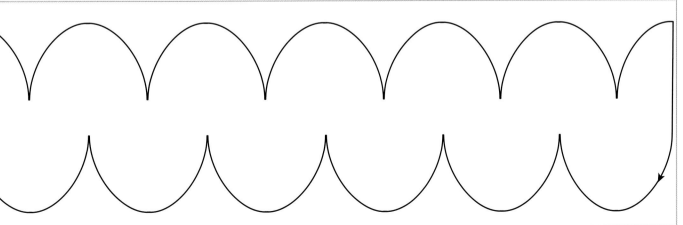

Ribbon Candy

DESIGNED BY CHRISTA WATSON

The figure-eight shape squishes nicely into corners, borders, and sashing strips and provides lots of texture with minimal effort. The irregularity of the shapes makes them easy to quilt without marking. Start by quilting a rounded teardrop, and then stitching back and forth between the lines of the shape you wish to fill. When applying this texture to a larger block, supersize the figure eight or quilt stacked rows to fill in the space. Vary the size of the stacked rows as desired.

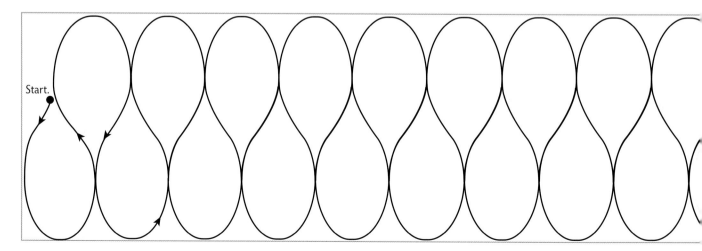

Start.

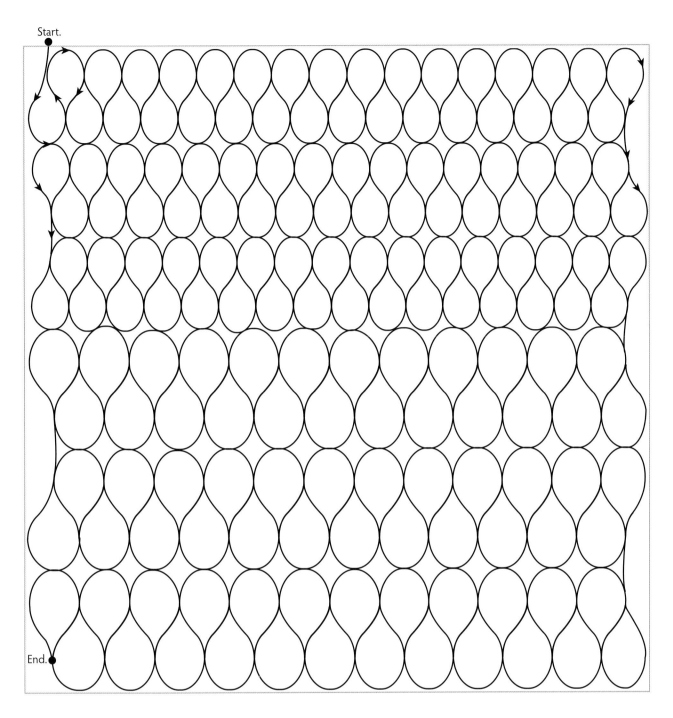

End.

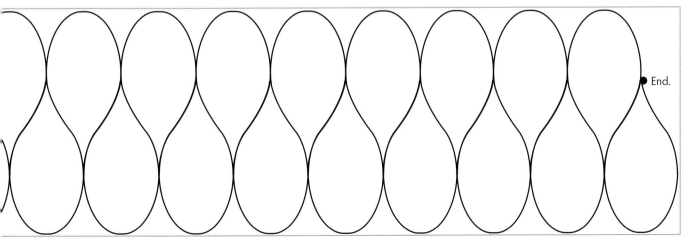

End.

Double Eights

DESIGNED BY VICKI RUEBEL

Double Eights is a modified version of the single figure-eight design. Using different sizes of figure eights creates extra dimension and interest in the quilting and also adds a secondary diamond shape. This design works well for filling in borders, but it can be easily stacked, stretched out, or condensed to fit any area.

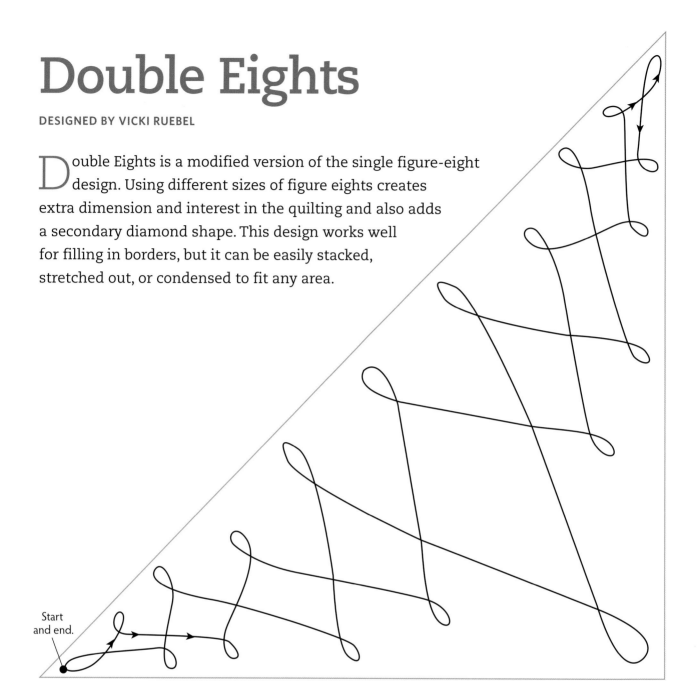

Start and end.

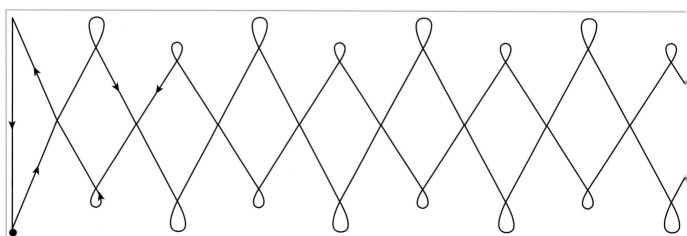

Start and end.

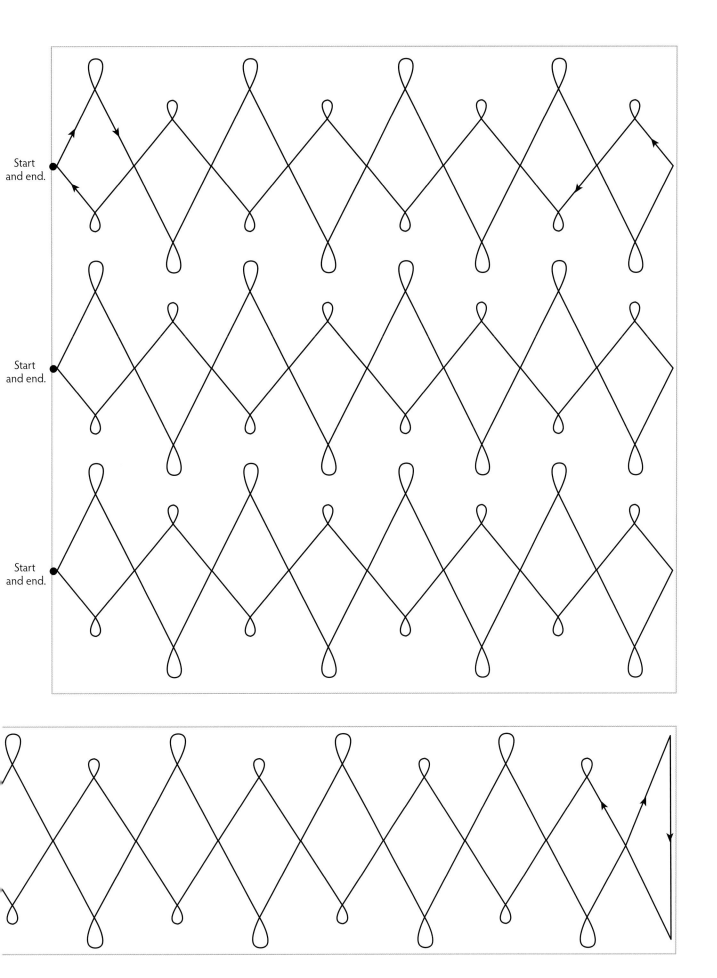

Start
and end.

Start
and end.

Start
and end.

Baby Bows

DESIGNED BY APRIL ROSENTHAL

Tiny figure eights parade around your quilt in this easy-to-master design. The key to getting it right is stitching crisp transitions: make sure you come to a full stop when changing directions at intersections so the bows remain curvy and the straight lines stay straight. On block corners and setting triangles, imagine drawing one of those giant gift bows in profile and you'll get it right every time.

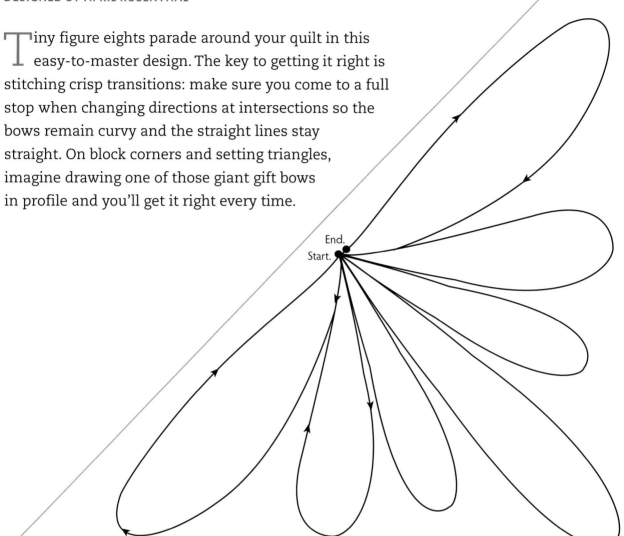

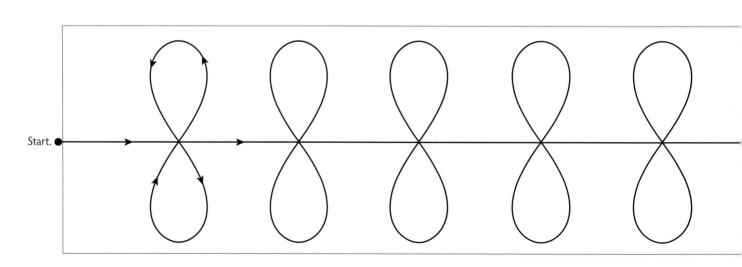

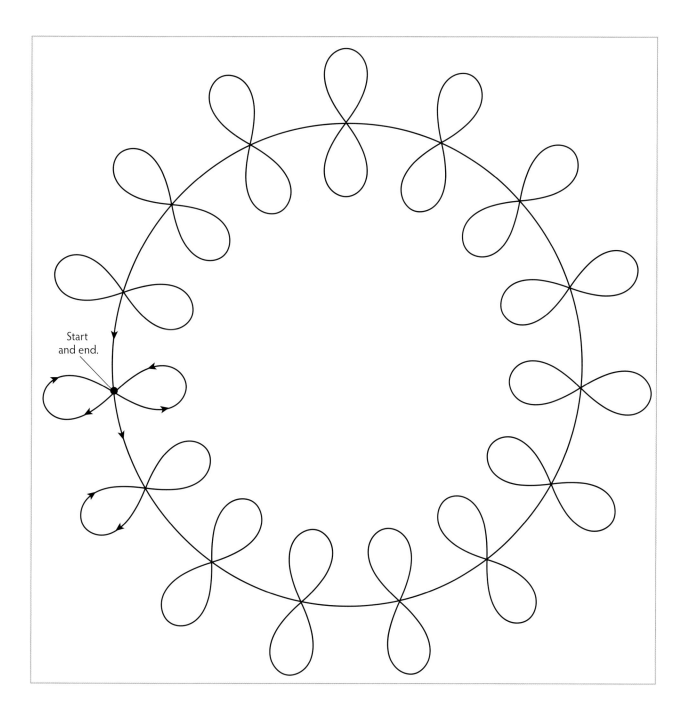

Start
and end.

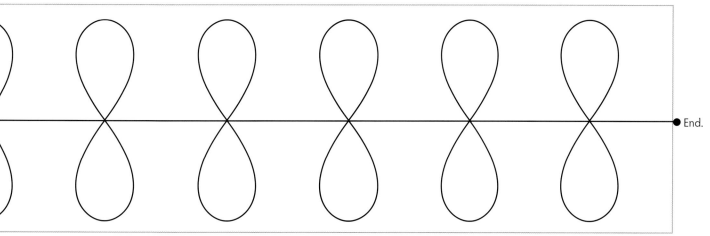

End.

Coils

DESIGNED BY CHRISTA WATSON

Coils are a fun and versatile option for filling many shapes on your quilt. For triangles, quilt smaller loops in the corners and larger loops toward the center. In a border, vary the shape of the loops as shown or make them all the same size for a different look. In a square, first quilt or mark an X from corner to opposite corner. Then fill the block with continuous coils in sections, working clockwise around the block.

End.

Start.

Start.

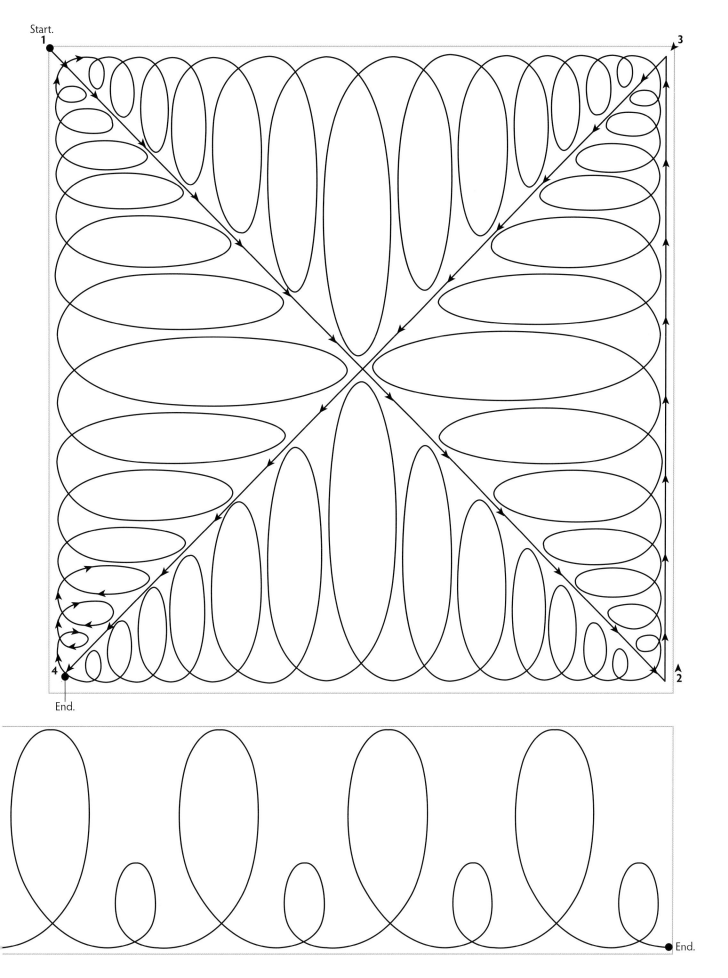

Easy Orange Peels

DESIGNED BY VICKI RUEBEL

The orange-peel motif, also known as a pumpkin seed, is a classic quilting design that's simple enough for beginners and works well in a variety of shapes. Orange peels look great scaled larger or smaller, depending on your preference for the shape you want to fill. Before quilting the orange peels, use a removable marking pen to draw a grid for a guide (as shown in blue).

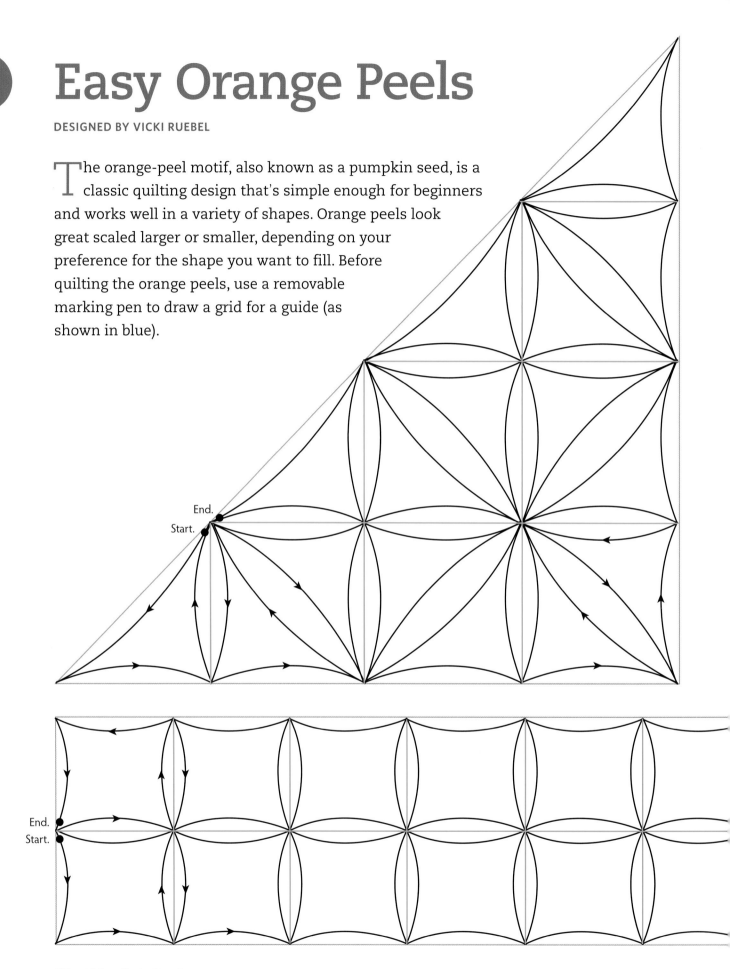

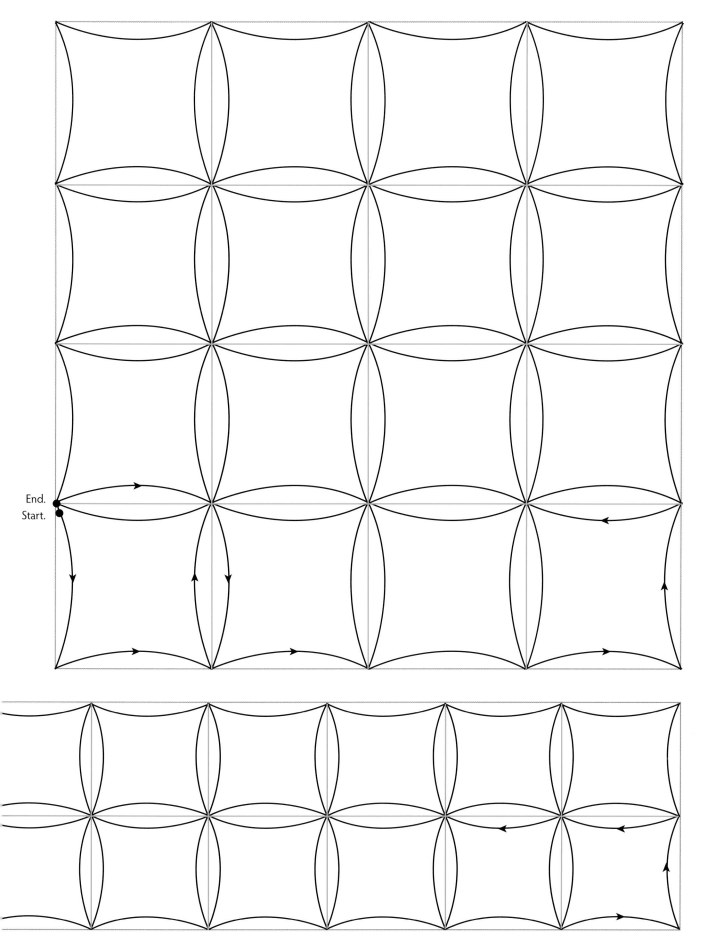

End.
Start.

Chevron Peel

DESIGNED BY APRIL ROSENTHAL

A simple update to the classic orange peel makes all the difference in this design. By adding a diagonal line across the center of the square, you can quilt the design without retracing, and you have the extra bonus of updating the look. This design is perfect for quilting postage-stamp designs and other quilts with lots of patchwork squares.

Start.

8

9

7

6

3

4

5

11

12

10

1

2

13

End.

Start.

1

4

8

5

9

10

7

2

3

6

Start.

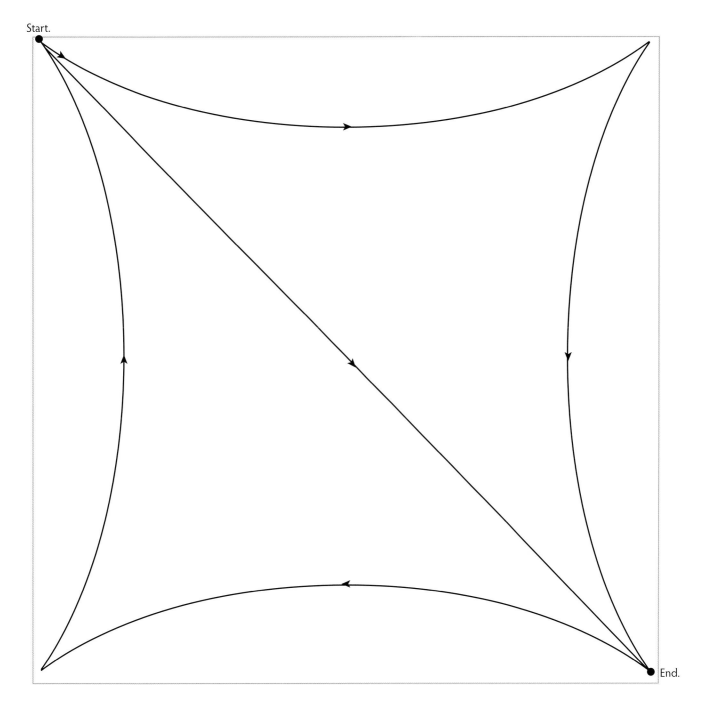

End.

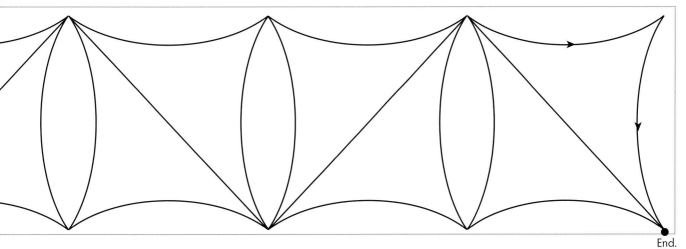

End.

Trumpets

DESIGNED BY VICKI RUEBEL

The trumpet is a simple echo design that works perfectly in triangles and adds an eye-catching geometric element to your quilt. Align or stack trumpets to quilt coordinating blocks and borders as shown. This design is fun for beginners and can be modified to have fewer or more echoes within the design as desired.

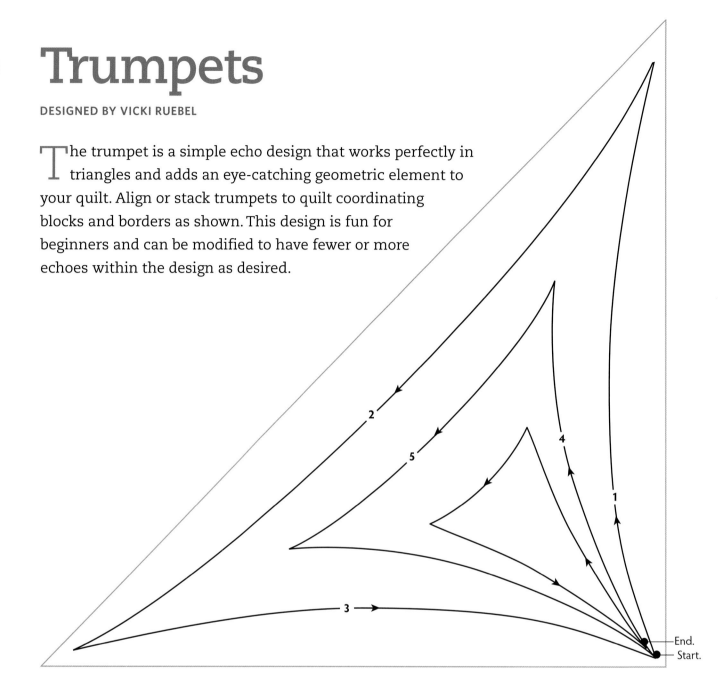

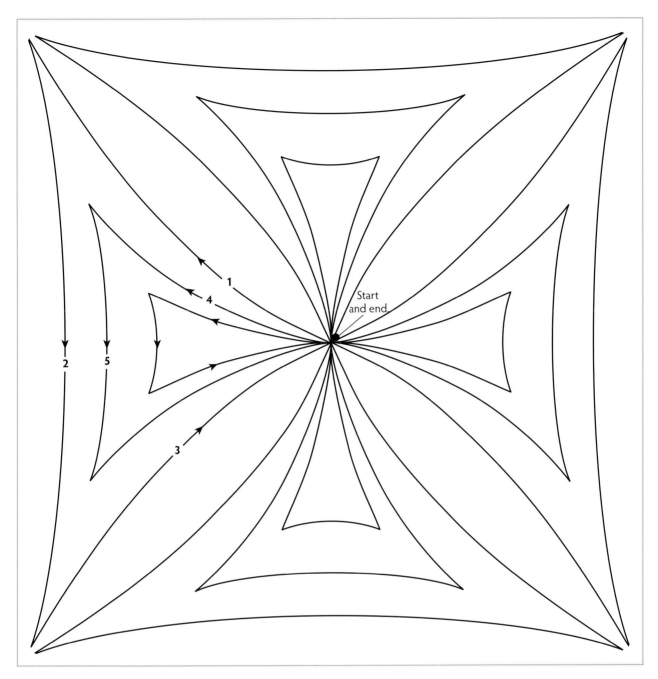

Start
and end.

1

4

2

5

3

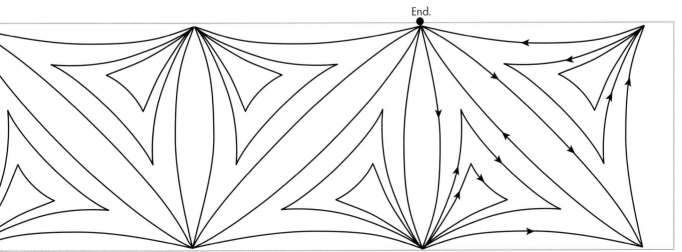

End.

Dizzy Paisley

DESIGNED BY SHEILA SINCLAIR SNYDER

This block design, a deconstructed paisley, begins with repeating curves accented by arching lines that echo toward the center to form a circle. For the block, stitch the outline first (black), and then fill the spaces with the echoing curved lines (blue). The setting triangle and border designs are also inspired by a deconstructed paisley. Using the design as a background fill on alternating rows of a quilt makes a big visual impact, so choose a thread color carefully. Select matching thread to add texture or a contrasting color for more pop.

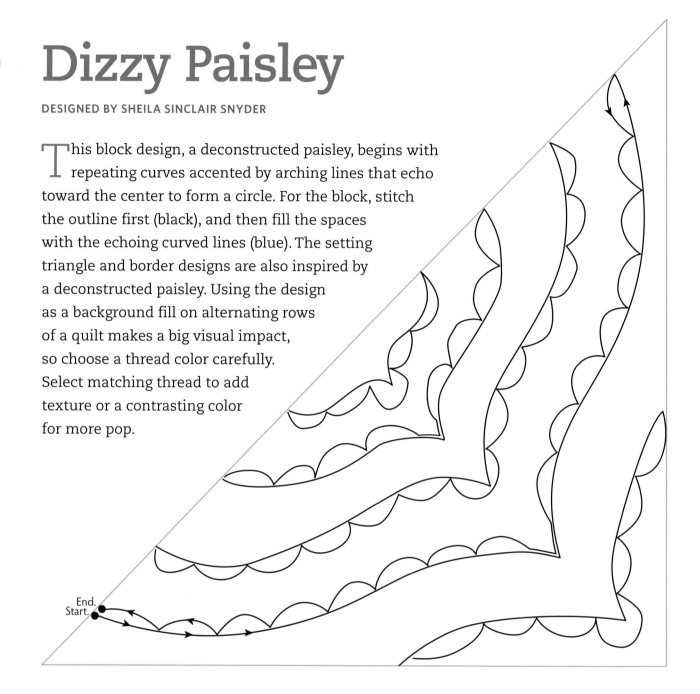

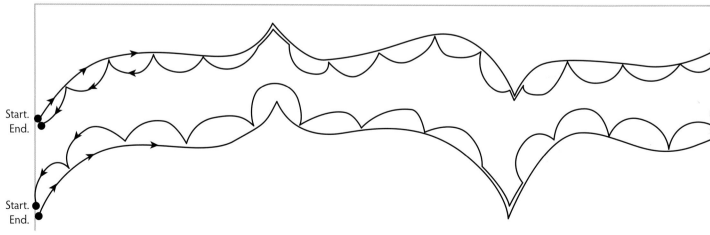

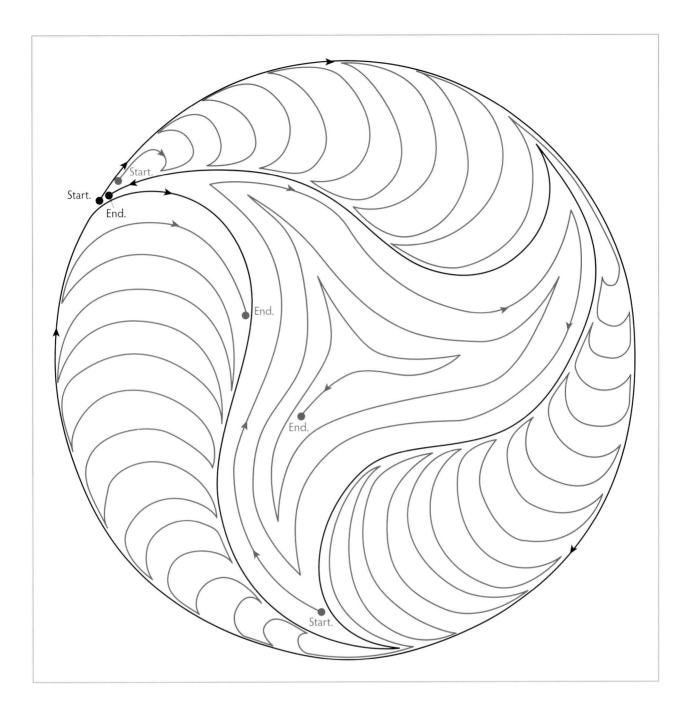

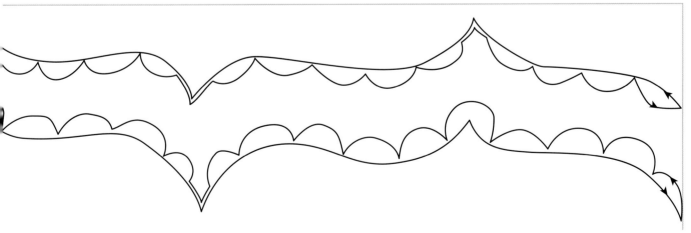

Boomerang

DESIGNED BY SHEILA SINCLAIR SNYDER

A boomerang is designed to circle around and return when tossed. This design may not return to its starting point, but is has a pleasing uniformity of spacing in the lines and curves, giving the illusion of returning. The design fills any space well and has a rhythm that gives your quilt a soft look and feel.

Start.

End.

Start.

End.

Start.

End.

Start.

End.

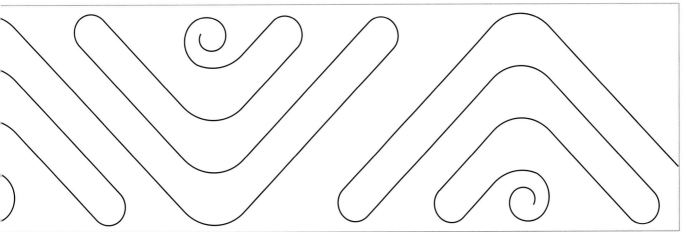

Swirly Whirly

DESIGNED BY APRIL ROSENTHAL

When learning to quilt this design, just imagine drawing the "@" symbol and you're nearly there! A simple tweak to a standard swirl design—crossing through the swirl rather than swirling out of it—makes for a different look and an easy motif to learn. When quilting the border design, alternate the place where you exit the swirls (top or bottom) for the fastest and most flowing movement.

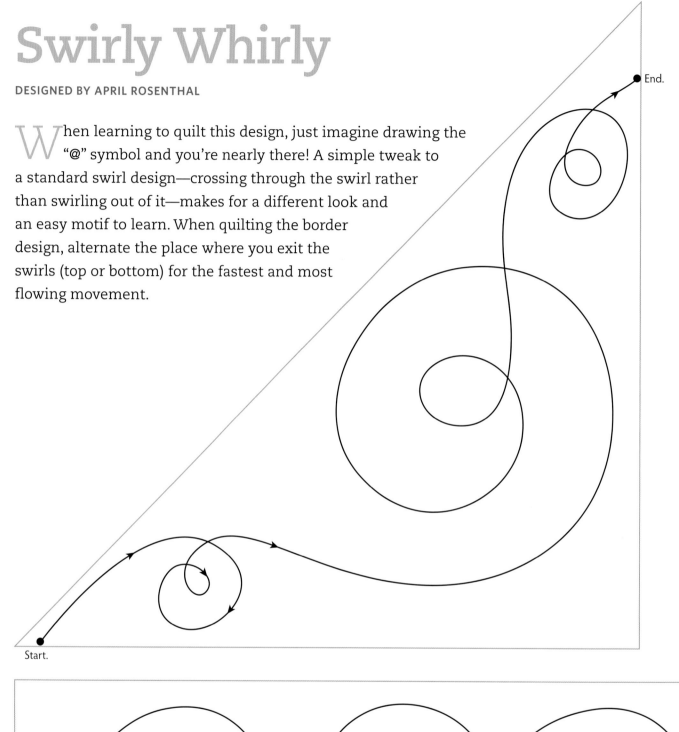

End.

Start.

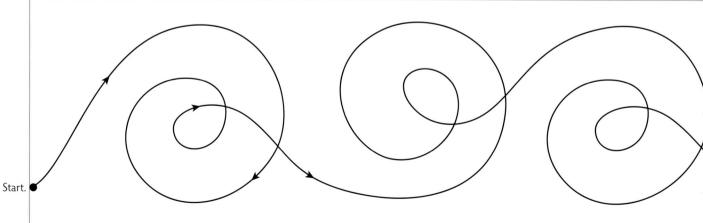

Start.

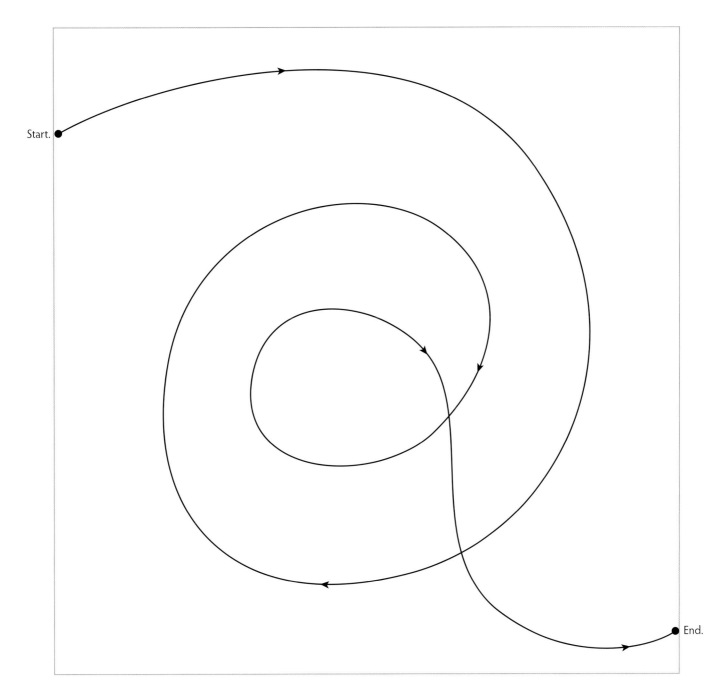

Start.

End.

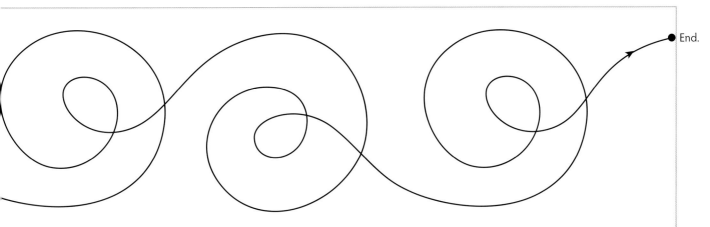

End.

I'll Always Olive You

DESIGNED BY MADDIE KERTAY

A playful title fits this simple and whimsical circle-in-a-circle design that brings to mind olives on a branch. Scale the design up or down to fit the space as needed. The organic, no-pressure shape means that even if you aren't skilled at stitching perfect circles, you'll get a beautiful finish with this motif.

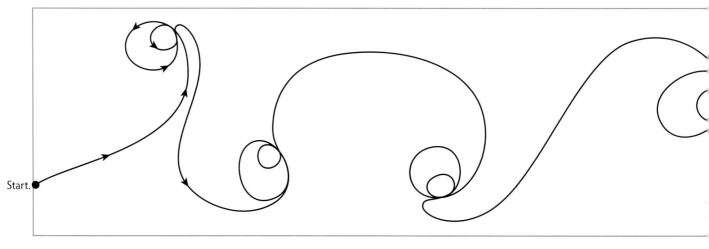

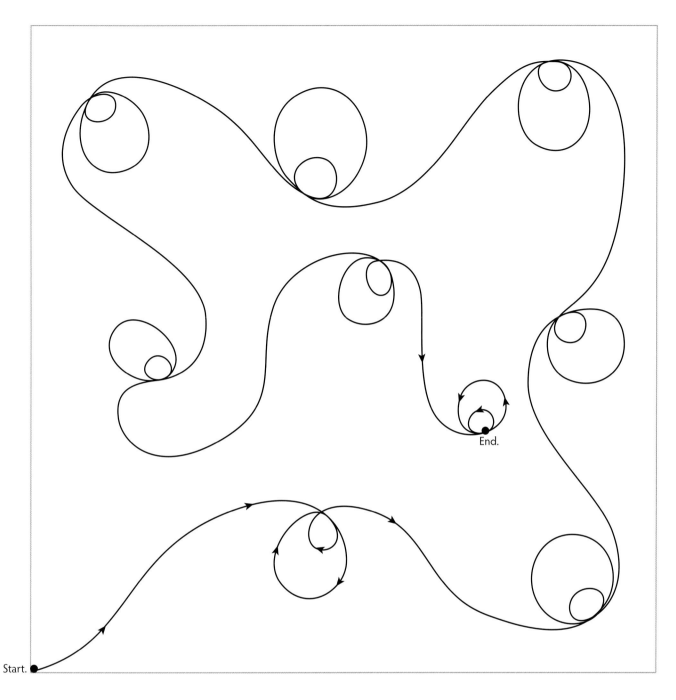

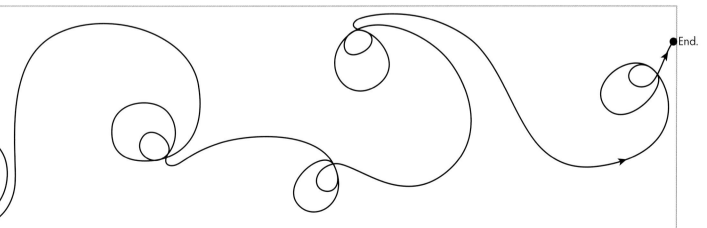

Fire Breather

DESIGNED BY APRIL ROSENTHAL

While one row of waves (or many rows going in the same direction) looks like water, alternating the horizontal orientation of the wave rows creates a fiery look. Fantastic as an overall design quilted in rows, as shown in the border below, or as an ornamental design in setting triangles, this fiery design is sure to add spice to your quilts.

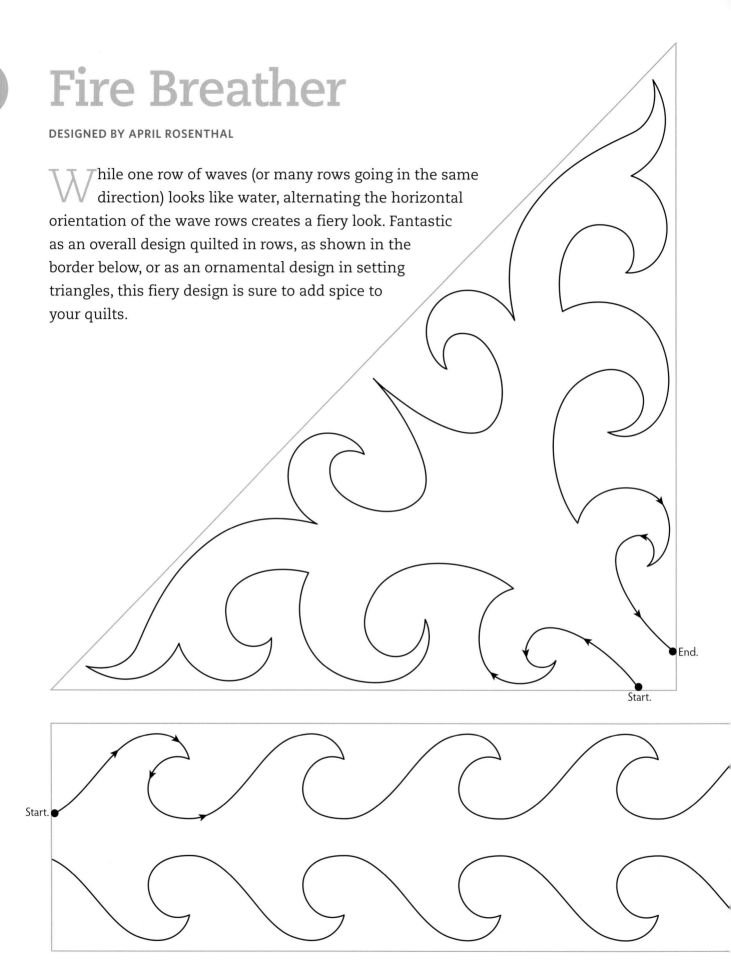

Start.

End.

End.

Whirlwind

DESIGNED BY ANGELA WALTERS

There's something so appealing about a gently curving serpentine line. It's an ideal option if you want to branch away from stitching a basic straight line without the stress of quilting swirls. These curvy designs create striking texture and are actually much easier to quilt than they might appear. If you're struggling with getting the spacing and curves right, practice doodling the designs a few times to get a feel for the flow.

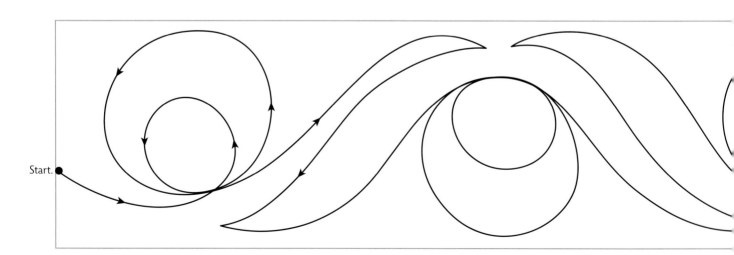

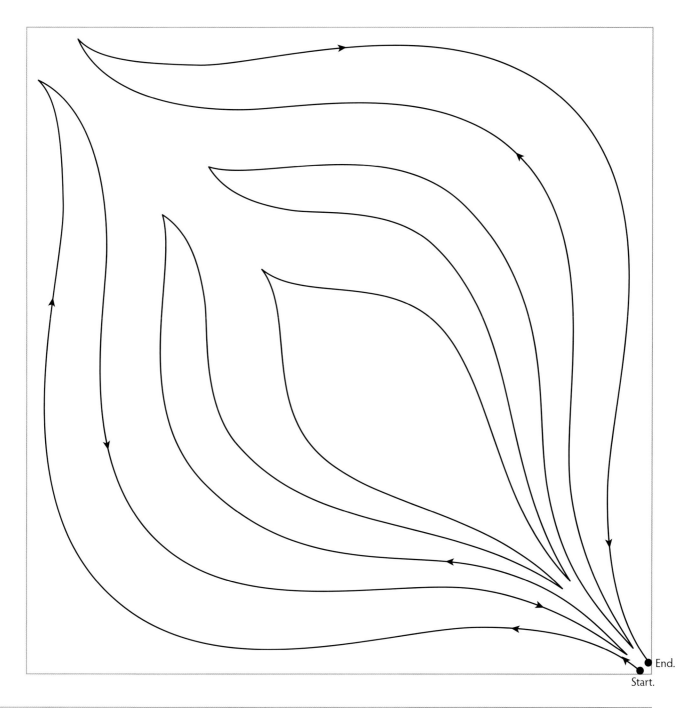

End.

Start.

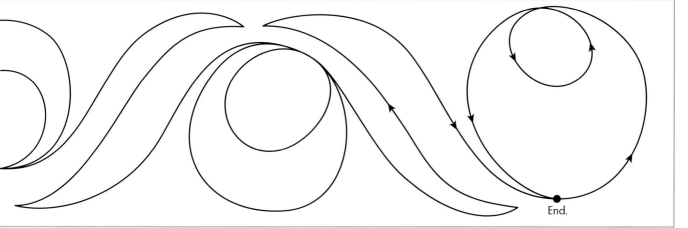

End.

Swirl and Curl

DESIGNED BY MELISSA CORRY

For this curvy design, stitch a large round shape that doesn't quite go full circle but rather swirls into the center approximately one and a half times. Stitch back out of the spiral, trying to keep an even distance between the two existing lines. Stitch past the start of the circle and make a curl. Stitch in the opposite direction of the curl to begin the next swirl. For any spaces that are too small for a full swirl, use a simple curl.

End.

Start.

End.

Swirled Paisley

DESIGNED BY MELISSA CORRY

Swirled Paisley adds an extra touch to the Swirl and Curl design on page 68. Start by stitching a Swirl and Curl, but add a large teardrop shape that ends in a point. Then echo stitch inside the teardrop twice, making the shape smaller toward the center. Travel along the outside edge of the paisley until you're ready to start a new swirl or paisley. Fill in small spaces with curls.

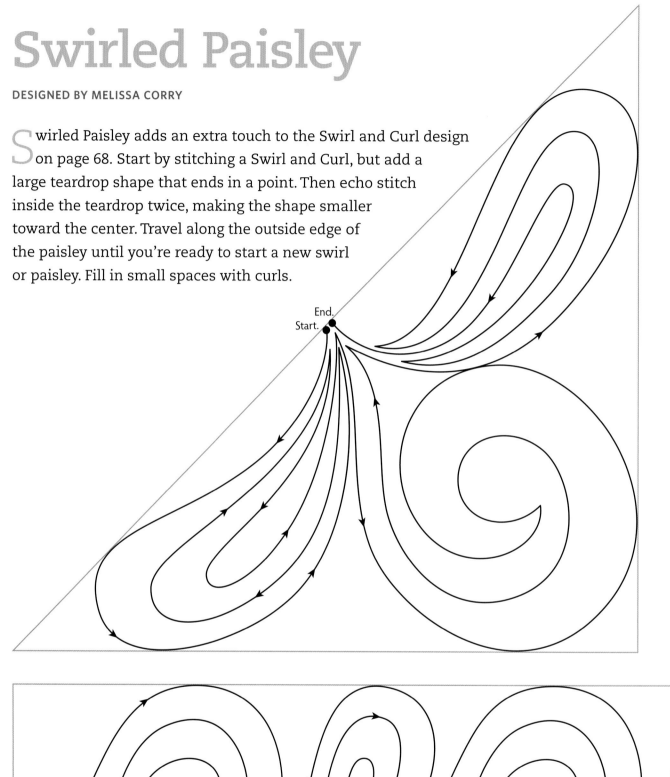

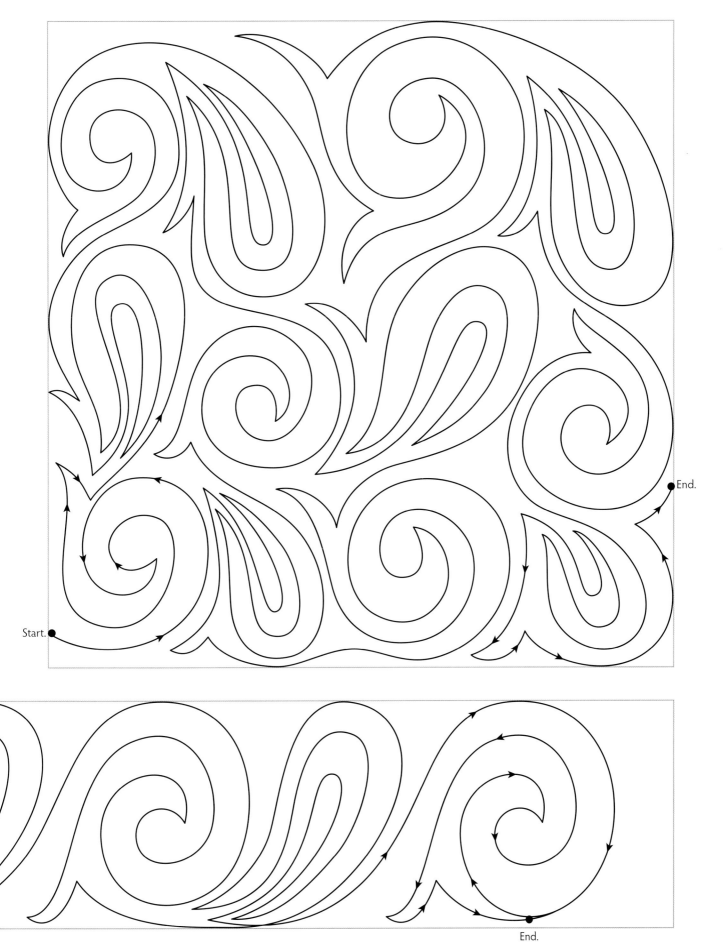

Start.

End.

End.

Swirled-and-Pebbled Paisley

DESIGNED BY MELISSA CORRY

Swirled-and-Pebbled Paisley builds from the Swirled Paisley design on page 70 and adds pebbling for an extra pop. Follow the process for the Swirled Paisley design, but fill in small spaces with pebbles rather than curls. The pebbles look great in a line or a cluster. Stitch the pebbles using your desired method (see page 7 for examples), retracing as needed to move around the space.

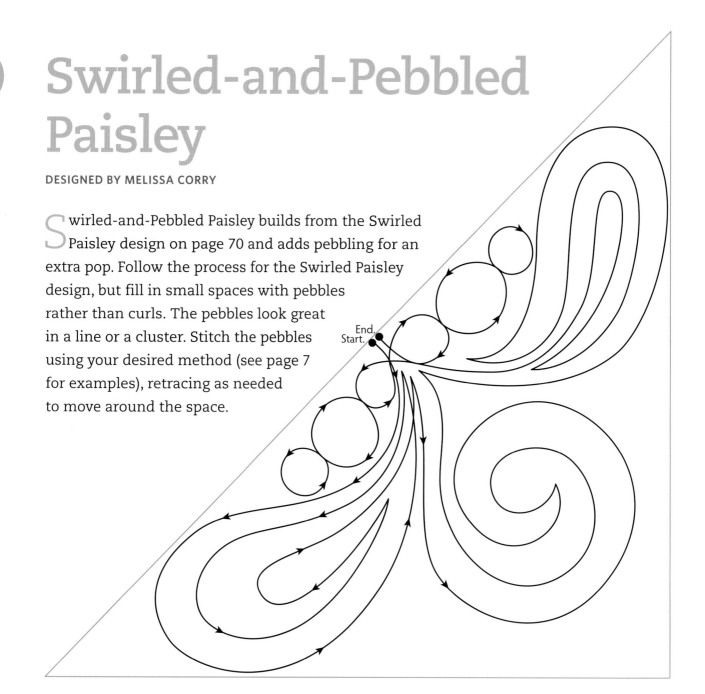

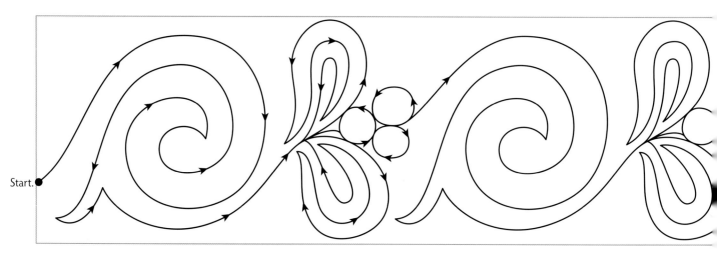

Start.

End.

End.

Swirls and Pebbles

DESIGNED BY MADDIE KERTAY

The Swirls and Pebbles design is all about playing with scale. The pebbles are the element that really sets off the design, so don't be shy in adding them. While the design is dense overall, stitching larger swirls will take up more space and make the design a bit looser if you prefer. Stitch pebbles to move from one swirl to the next. On the border, work the swirl first, and then echo the shape. Fill in the empty spaces with pebbles to make the swirls pop.

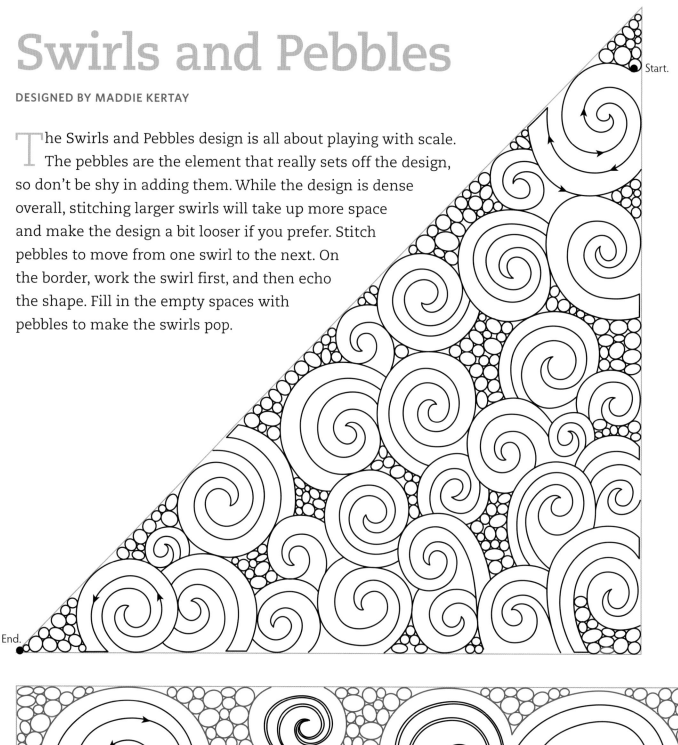

End.

Start.

Swirlmania

DESIGNED BY VICKI RUEBEL

Swirls are one of the most versatile quilting designs. They fit well in any shape, making it simple to move in and out of corners. On each shape, stitch into and out of the center of the swirl, backtracking on top of the previously stitched line. The first swirl is highlighted in red so you can see how the design is formed. After quilting the main swirls, as shown in black, fill the spaces around the swirls with echoing curves, as shown in blue.

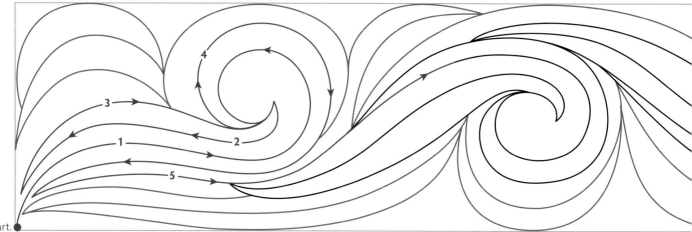

Start.

End.

1 2 3 4 5

End.

Curly Q

DESIGNED BY KAREN M. BURNS

The Curly Q design is one of Karen's favorites. It's great for beginners but can also be combined with other doodling designs to give it a more intricate or advanced look. Be adventuresome as you play with this design, as it does play well with others! Try changing the size or adding more curls as you doodle. Curly Q works as both an allover design and in distinct shapes, such as the block, border, and triangle.

End.

Start.

Start.

Start.

End.

End.

Feathered Swirl

DESIGNED BY MELISSA CORRY

The Feathered Swirl starts in the same way as the Swirl and Curl design on page 68. Stitch a swirl and a curl, but bring the curl back to touch the outside of the swirl. Then stitch a feather by creating an arched half-circle shape, curving back again to touch the outside swirl. Repeat the feathers as far as you like around the swirl, and then echo the feathers. For the triangle design, first stitch the flower, and then fill the corners with echoing curves.

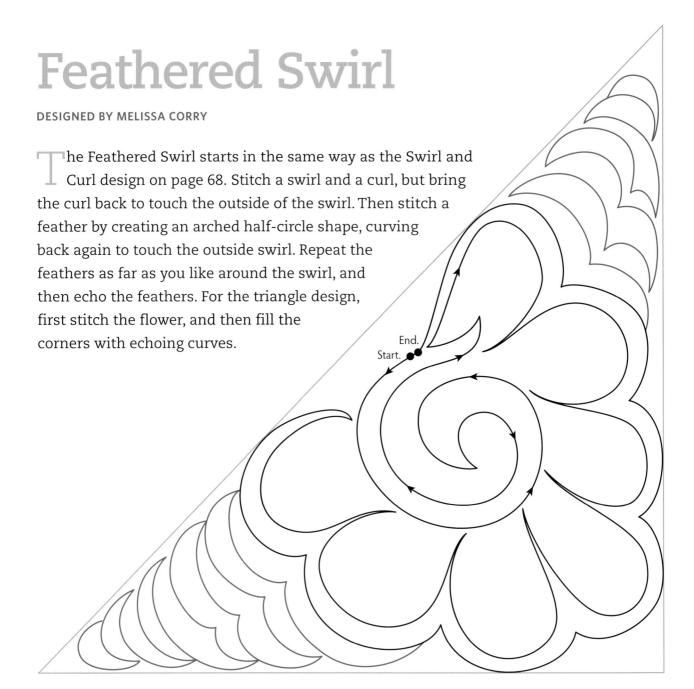

End.

Start.

End.

Simple Feather

DESIGNED BY VICKI RUEBEL

A classic motif, the feather adds graceful movement to quilts. The plumes of feathers can be easily manipulated to fit any shape as needed. To add even more interest, alternate the direction of the feathers as shown in the border design. On the triangle and border, stitch the plumes on one side of the center spine. Then backtrack on top of the spine and stitch the plumes on the other side of the spine. The blue arrows indicate where to backtrack as you stitch.

Start.

End.

End.

Fancy Hook Feathers

DESIGNED BY VICKI RUEBEL

Fancy Hook Feathers have a more intricate look than the Simple Feather on page 82, giving a whimsical touch to your quilt. The hook design eliminates the need for backtracking and adds detail to each plume. You can break up borders by quilting feathers to fill a triangle, as shown below, before moving on to the next portion of the border. As you can see, the shape of the plumes is ideal for triangles. To stitch uniform feathers in the border, draw a guideline using a removable pen (as shown in blue).

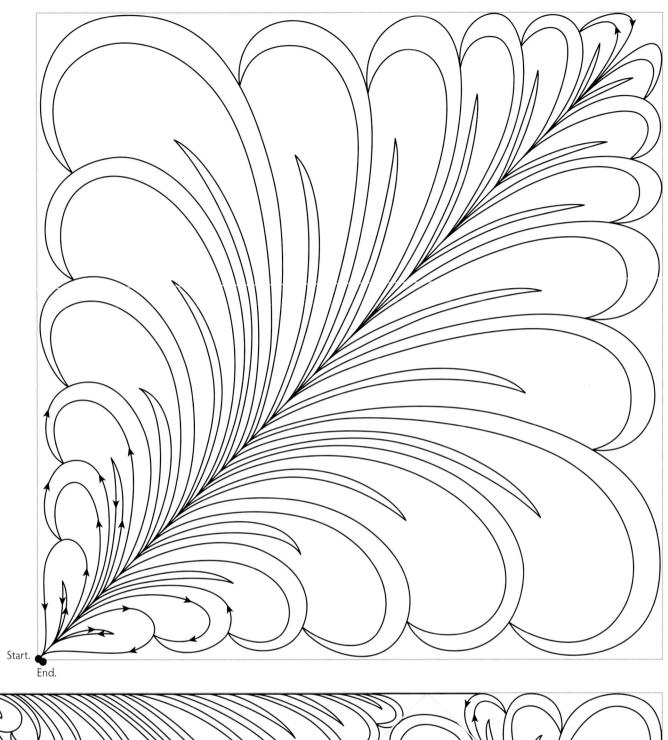

Start.
End.

Swirling Plumes

DESIGNED BY VICKI RUEBEL

In this feather variation, the plumes that radiate from a central swirl can be stretched to fill in small spaces and corners. The hook design eliminates backtracking and hides many imperfections. You can use Swirling Plumes to add movement to a border, or modify the motif to create a stunning allover quilt design. Begin with the central swirl shape, and then stitch the plumes around the swirl.

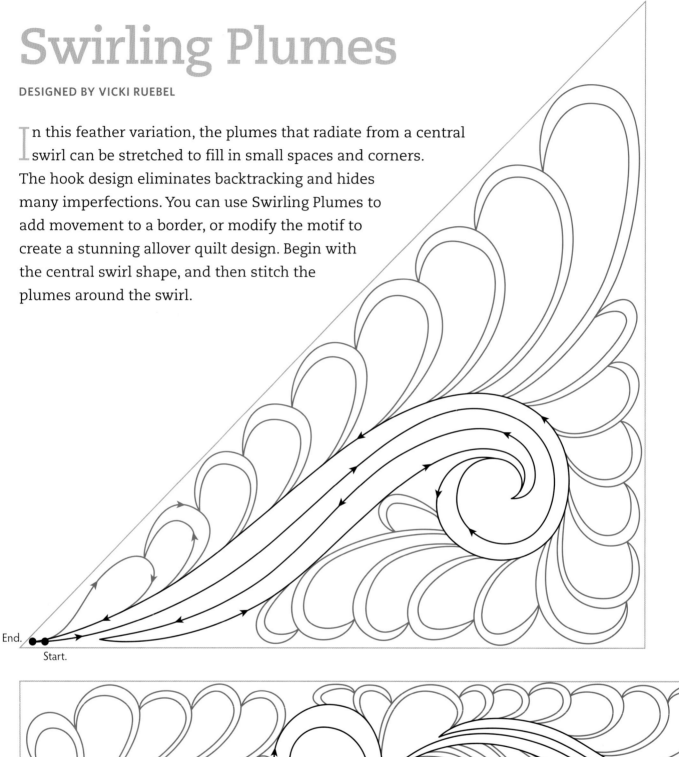

Start.

End.

End.

Start.

End.

Feather Boa

DESIGNED BY APRIL ROSENTHAL

Feather patterns are more fun with some fluff! Add a second loop to each feather to create an ornate look that's sure to wow. Consider drawing a guideline with chalk or other temporary marker to notate where the spine of the Feather Boa should be (as shown in blue). Doing so will give you a reference point for starting and stopping each feather. Note that you'll be stitching along the spine as you continue making loops.

Start and end.

Start and end.

Start and end.

Leaf Frond

DESIGNED BY KAREN M. BURNS

Karen often uses a leaf frond as an alternative to a classic feather, especially on quilts that have a leafy or botanical design. As you stitch, vary the size of the leaf as needed to fill the space. Alternate stitching the leaves on each side of the vine, and then stitch the vein of each leaf. Or if you prefer, stitch all the leaves on one side of the spine, and then stitch the leaves on the other side in the opposite direction. Backtrack along the spine as needed to stitch each leaf. This design gets even better with practice!

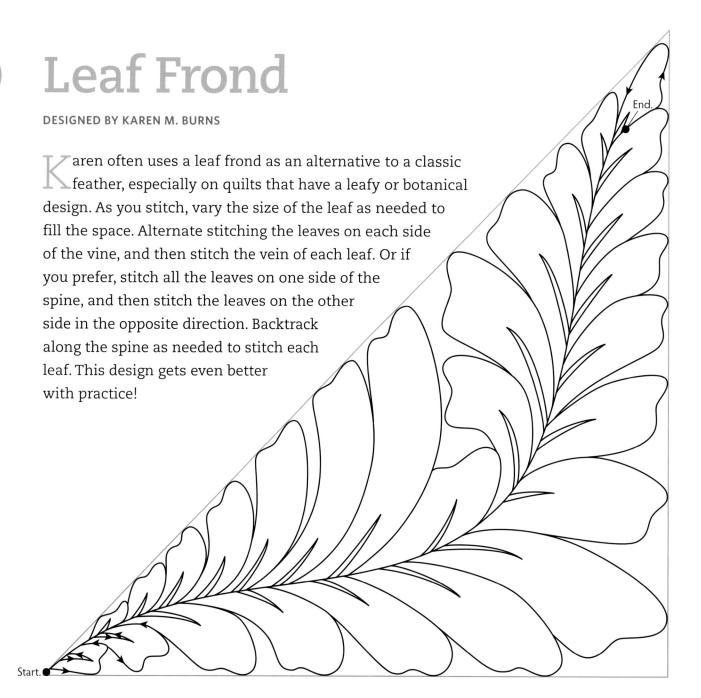

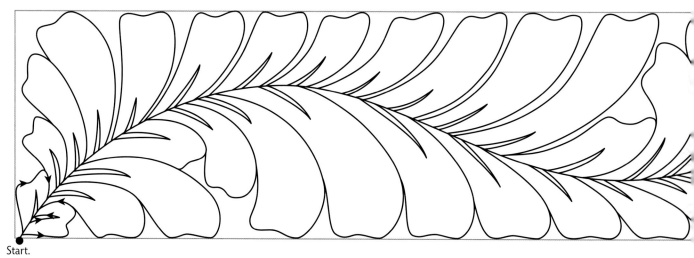

End.

Start.

End.

Fancy Floral

DESIGNED BY APRIL ROSENTHAL

These simple swirly blooms are ideal for any quilt that calls for an extra touch of sweetness. Practice doodling the design first to get a feel for how to stitch in and out of the flower shape. A large-scale blossom is a striking option for filling a block, and a chain of little blossoms looks lovely in a border. To fill in small spaces, such as the corners of the triangle, add curly leaves and vines. Keep stitching petals as needed to move smoothly from one motif to the next.

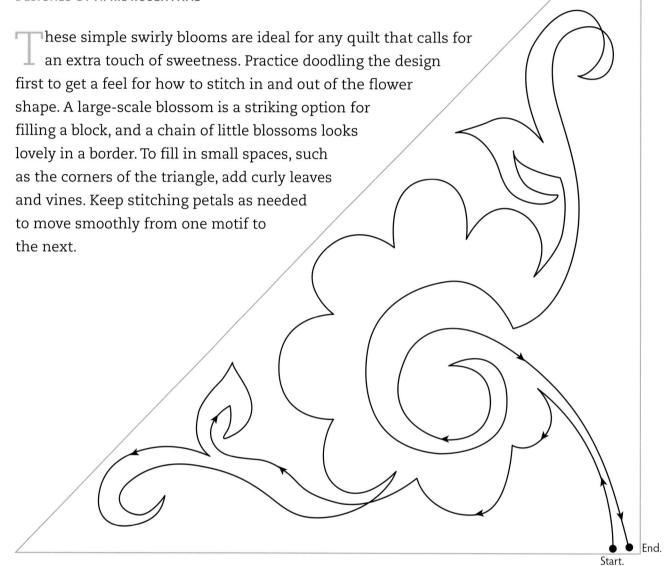

Start. End.

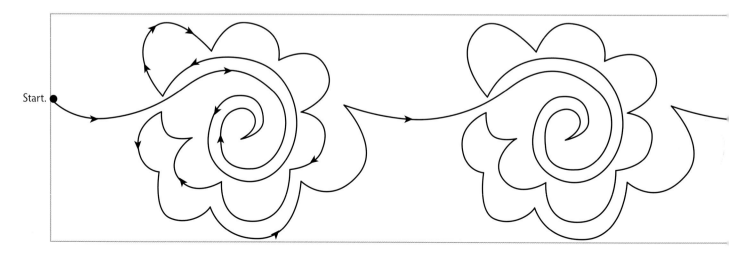

Start.

Start. End.

End.

Square Flower

DESIGNED BY LORI KENNEDY

This modern flower design beautifully fills any shape quickly, from squares to triangles to diamonds to circles. Begin with a center spiral, and then stitch outward to add squared-off petals to fill in the entire space. For a fuller look, add a center vein line to each petal and echo stitch the entire flower. To vary the design, offset the spiral and stitch longer and shorter petals.

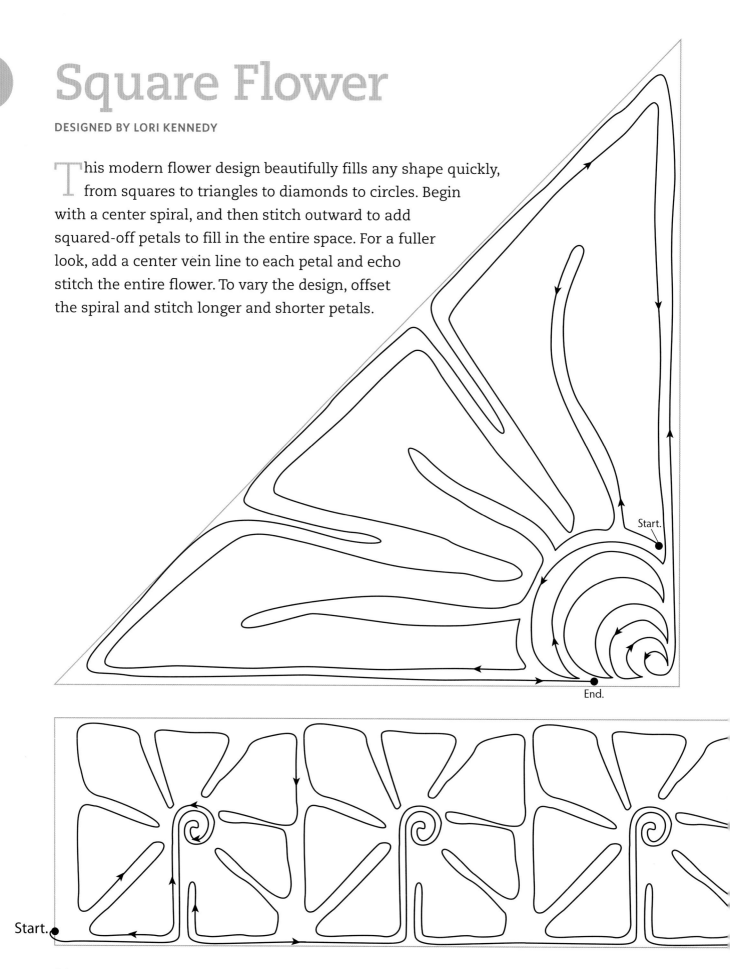

Spools of Thread

DESIGNED BY LORI KENNEDY

This motif gives you the perfect way to add your own personality and love of stitching to your next quilt. Add just a single spool in the corner with your signature, or design a border of spools. Create each spool with a different design, such as scallops or zigzags, and then stitch a looped line to begin the next spool. For a fun touch, write a message in the unspooled line of thread, such as "A stitch in time saves nine" or "Stitched with love."

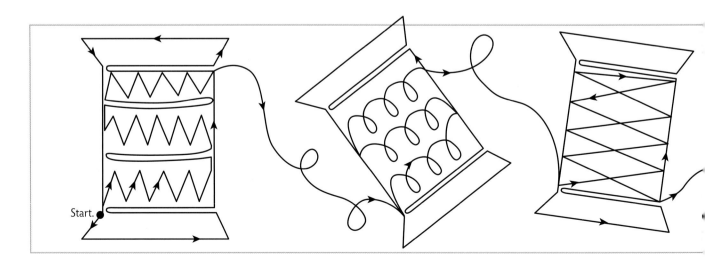

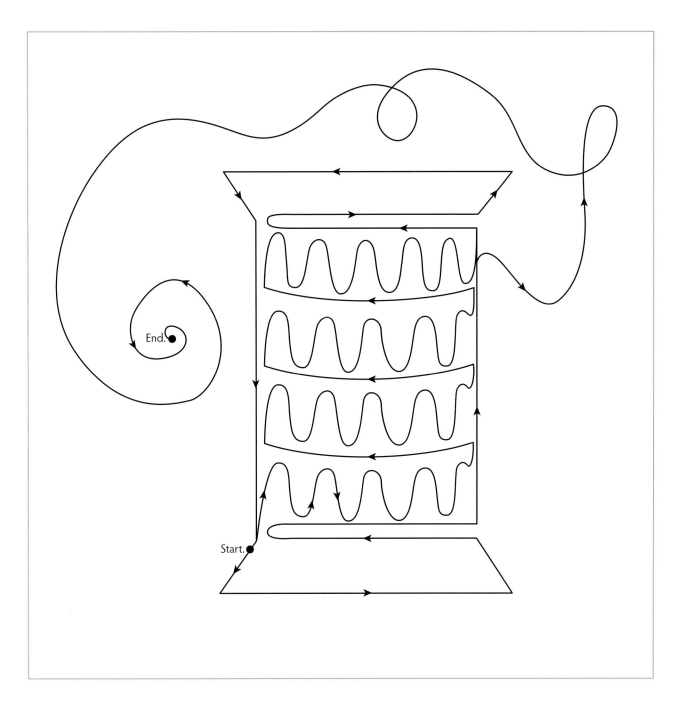

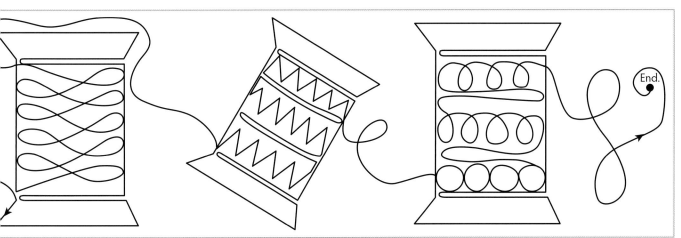

Peas in a Pod

DESIGNED BY MADDIE KERTAY

Peas in a Pod is a sweet meandering filler design. As you switch the direction of the pea pods to fill the space you're working in, add some swirls as needed for balance. First align the outer pod, inner pod, and peas, and then stitch the swirls to fill in leftover spaces.

Start and end at center.

End.

Hipster Holly

DESIGNED BY MADDIE KERTAY

Holiday quilts need not be stuffy affairs! Use this fast and flowing design; it makes the most of a bump and curve pattern, forming holly and berries that will dress up just about any winter quilt. The swirls and loose spirals keep the festive look airy and open.

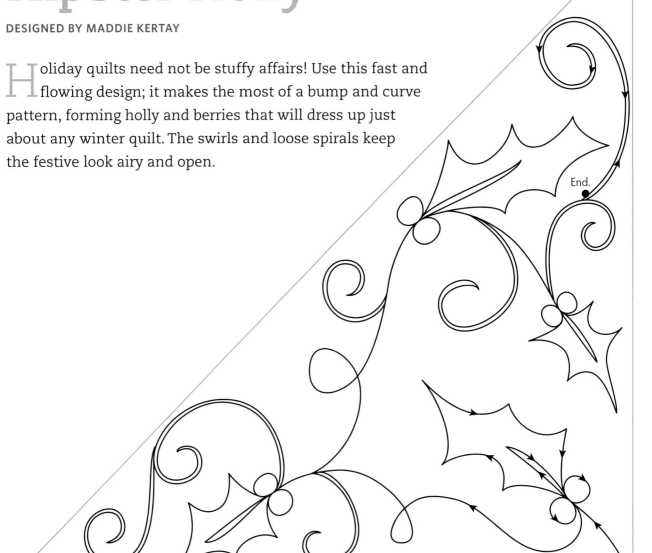

Start and end.

End.

Way to Snow

DESIGNED BY MADDIE KERTAY

Way to Snow is part of Maddie's design series in which a water-soluble blue pen provides the subtle direction needed to form the motifs. Before stitching, plot out the circle and six dots for each snowflake as shown in blue. Form the snowflakes around each set of markings. Using this method, the snowflakes will be consistently spaced yet loose and organic to add just the right touch to your holiday quilts.

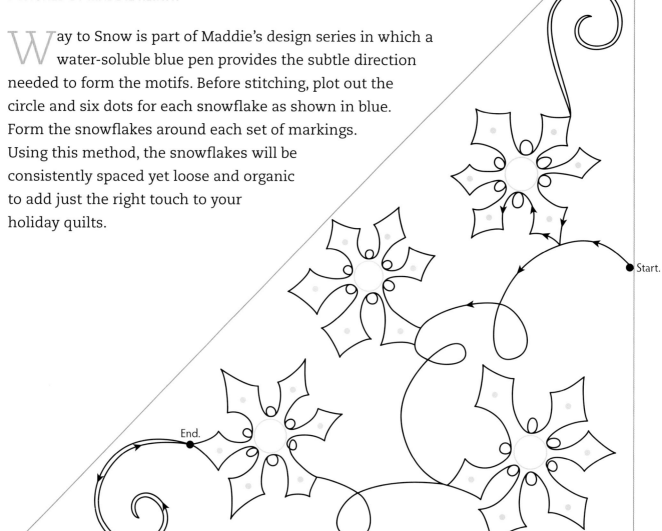

Petal Pusher

DESIGNED BY APRIL ROSENTHAL

Pointed petals can be used in many different ways for a variety of stunning designs. Consider using them as isolated flowers in a border, starting them in the center and radiating outward to fill a block. Or place them randomly for a "fallen leaves" look. The key to pointed petals is making a full stop at the tip of the petal, so there's a single stitch between direction changes.

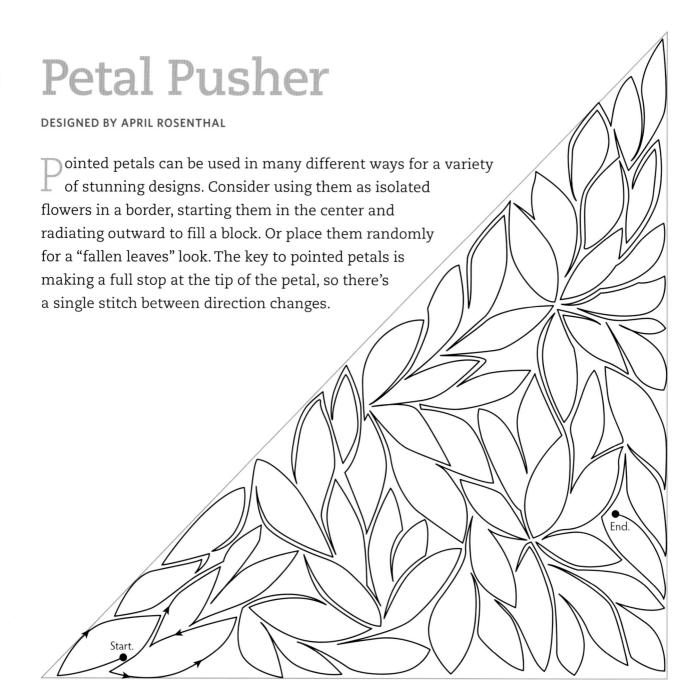

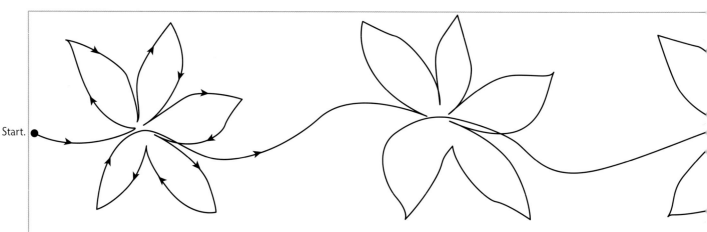

Leaf It to Me

DESIGNED BY MADDIE KERTAY

Leaf It to Me is a great option for fall-themed quilts where you want foliage to be the star. With the ability to place the leaves in any direction, you can use this design as a flexible fill for many shapes. The vine curl can help fill spots that would be too busy if another leaf were added. Note that you'll be retracing veins and vines in order to continue to the next motif.

Fireworks

DESIGNED BY MELISSA CORRY

Add an energetic burst to your quilt with the simple Fireworks design. To form the motifs, first stitch a straight line, and then stitch a group of spikes radiating up and straight outward from the line. Continue making spikes to form a half-circle grouping of points. When the half-circle is complete, stitch a straight line away from the motif, far enough away to begin a new Firework. To finish the shape, repeat the motion in the opposite direction, filling in the second half of the circled spikes.

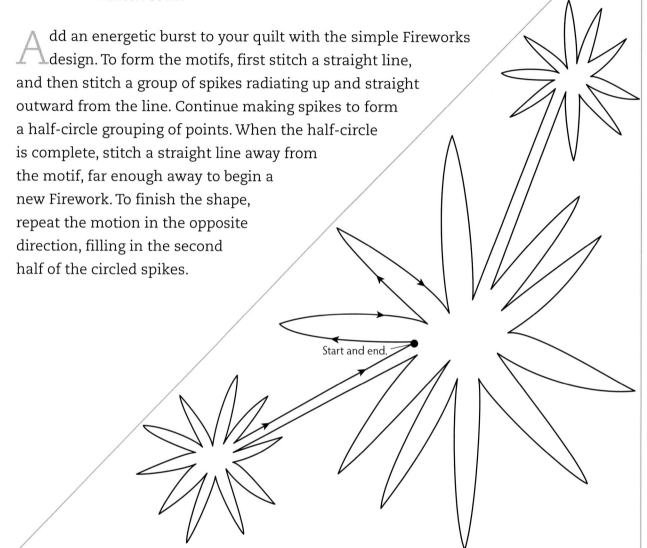

Start and end.

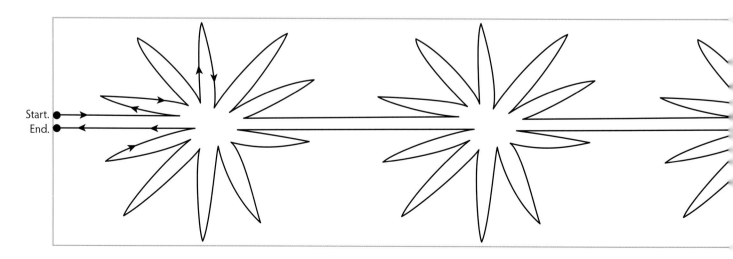

Start.
End.

Start.

End.

Spotlight

DESIGNED BY SHEILA SINCLAIR SNYDER

A little ruler work is all it takes to create this wonderful geometric design that brings to mind a shining spotlight. The angular shapes add many diagonal lines that draw the eye from point to point across the quilt, and the gently curved ribbons bring out an appealing contrast. For the block design, stitch the ribbons after the geometric shapes.

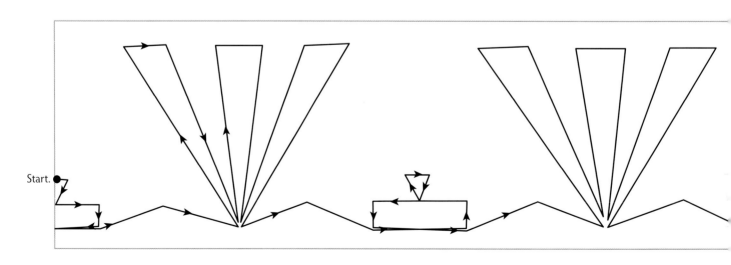

Start and end.

Start and end.

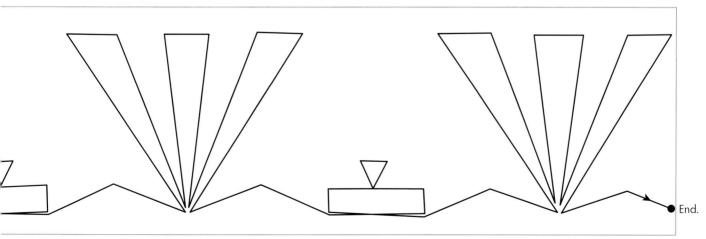

End.

Spiral Heart

DESIGNED BY LORI KENNEDY

The fast and fabulous Spiral Heart is a classic motif that suits modern and traditional quilts alike. Stitch right and left spirals to create the heart shape, and then add any embellishment in the center, such as the modified kite shape shown or your own initials! To create the border motif, stitch the right and left spirals and leave a slight gap between them to begin stitching the next heart in the chain. This method prevents an excessive buildup of stitches.

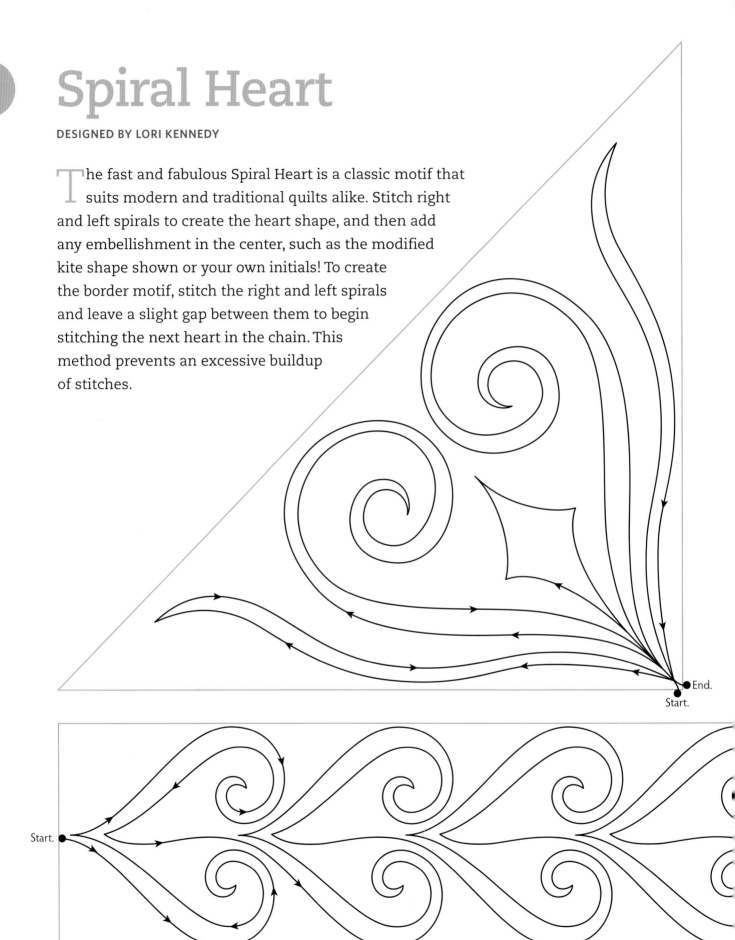

Start. End.

End.

Good Day Sunshine

DESIGNED BY MADDIE KERTAY

Bold but easy, this sunflower surrounded by spirals makes for an impressive motif, especially when you know how easy it is to create. First stitch the center circle and crosshatching. Then stitch the petals and echo a shadow line. Fill in the surrounding area with swirls. Adjust the number of swirls, as well as the tightness or looseness of the swirls, according to the density you want in this design.

Start and end shadow line.

Start and end shadow line.

Curves Ahead

DESIGNED BY ANGELA WALTERS

Clamshell quilting designs have been around almost as long as quilting itself. While they may seem outdated to some, clamshells can be easily tweaked to form interesting variations. Playing with the placement of the curves, adding a fun teardrop detail, and combining them with free-motion quilting results in fun designs that work on any kind of quilt.

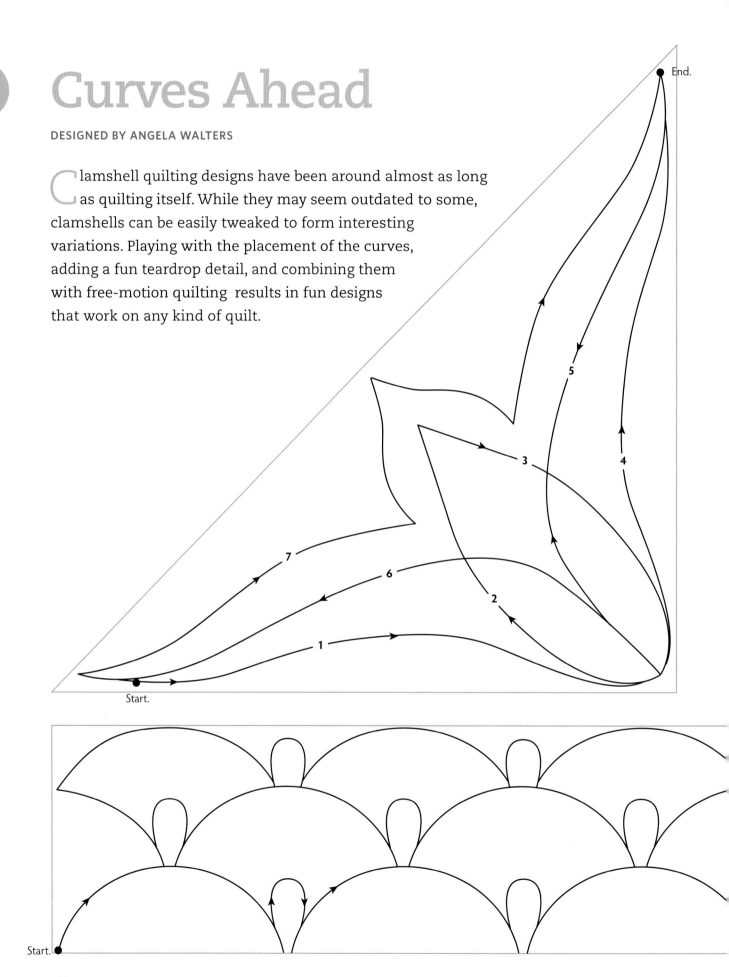

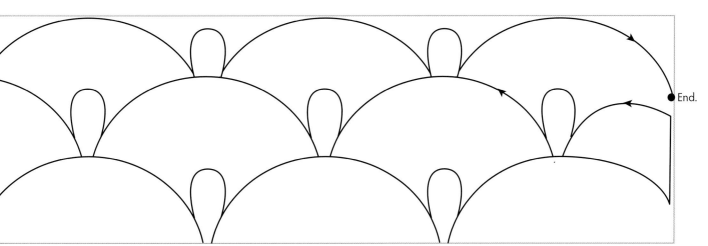

Claire's Rose

DESIGNED BY LORI KENNEDY

Claire's Rose is a beautiful flower motif that's simple enough for beginning quilters to tackle. Start with a spiral center, and then add scallops, echo stitching each scallop before adding another round of scallops. This design looks great in small spaces and can be easily adapted to larger shapes by adding additional rows of scallops. Use pointed leaves to fill in corners.

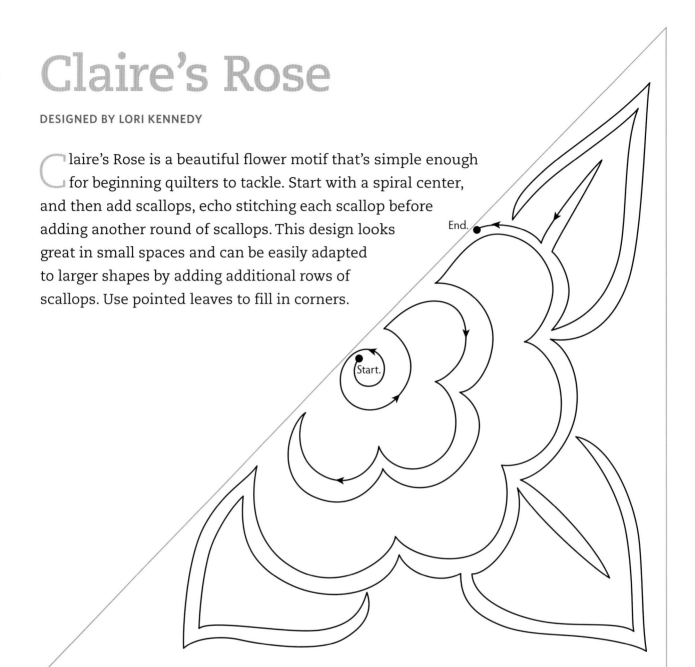

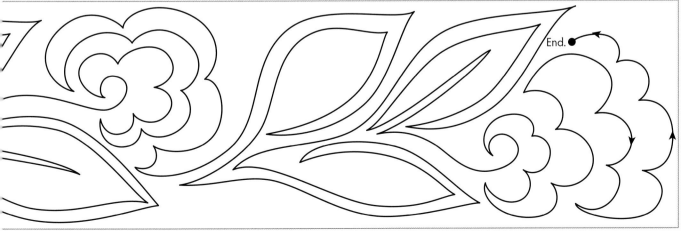

Frame It!

DESIGNED BY VICKI RUEBEL

Add texture and interest to any quilt with this design. The tight back-and-forth lines frame an orange-peel motif, while feathers in the corners soften the look. This structured shape adds interest by breaking up large areas, and the feathers provide movement. Stitch the framed flower first, and then fill in the spaces with plumes. After stitching each plume, backtrack on top of the stitched line to start the next plume.

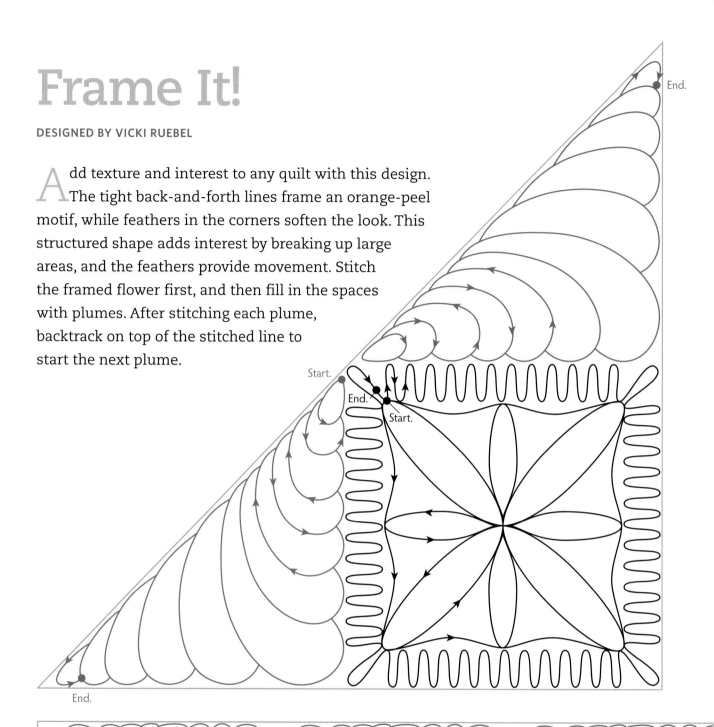

Start
and end.

Start and end.

Gone Fishing

DESIGNED BY SHEILA SINCLAIR SNYDER

The continuous-line fish in this block design are, believe it or not, a progression of paisley motifs. The fish-body shape and embellishments are similar to a classic paisley. Thread and fabric choices can easily give the design an Asian feel, or you can use different colors to create the look of a brook trout. To continue the aquatic theme, the setting triangle is a bubble design, and the border combines elements that represent a flowing stream. Stitch the echoing and waves (blue) after stitching the pebbles.

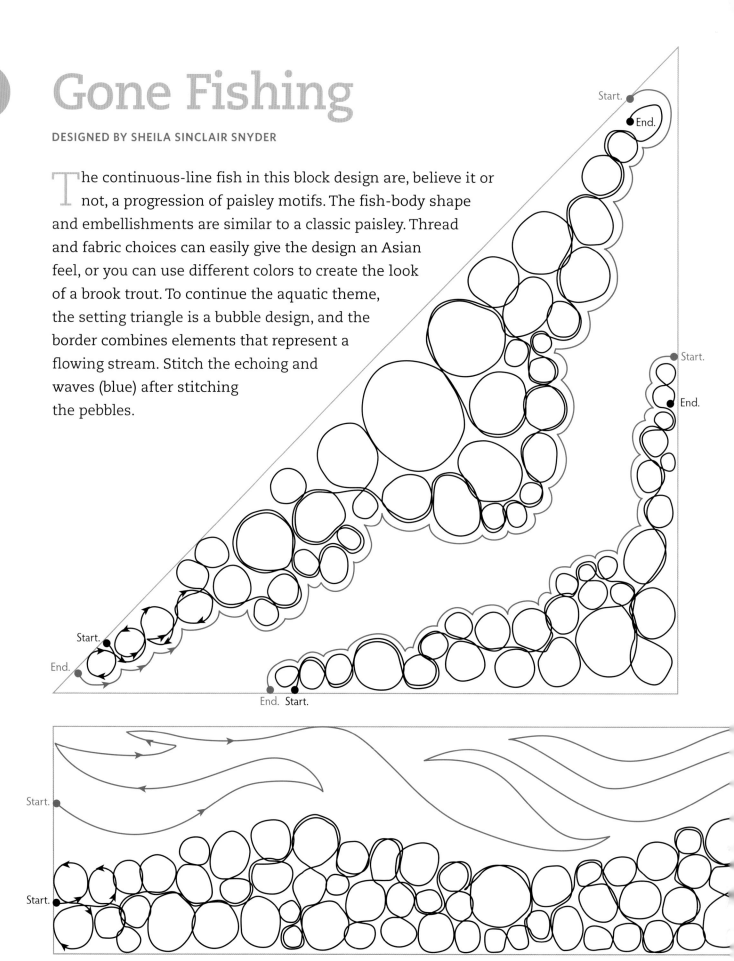

Start.

End.

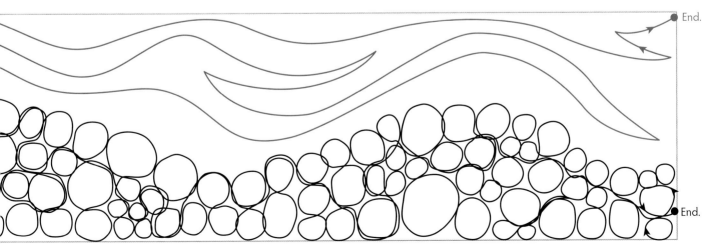

End.

End.

Posy Paisley

DESIGNED BY SHEILA SINCLAIR SNYDER

Whether paisleys form a wreath, fill a setting triangle, or are stretched into a border, the design is easily recognizable and well loved. Add a few embellishments to decorate an alternate block or setting triangle. There are countless options for thread color combinations and changes to increase the style factor. For the block and triangle, sew the paisley shapes, and then outline them in scallops. Fill the paisleys with the leaf motifs (blue).

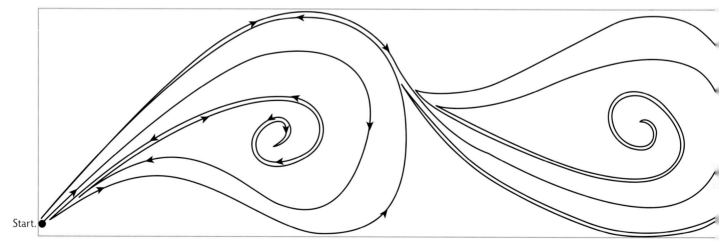

Start.

Start and end.

End.

Start.

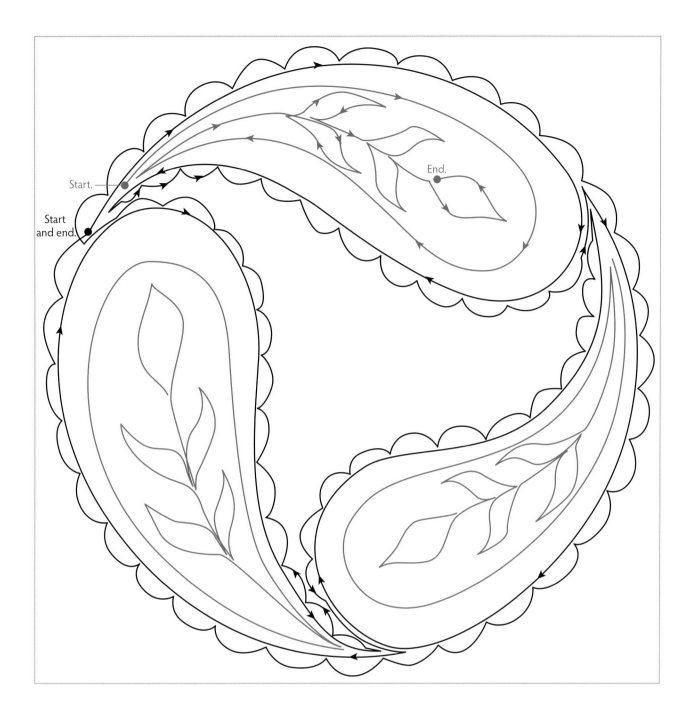

Start.

Start and end.

End.

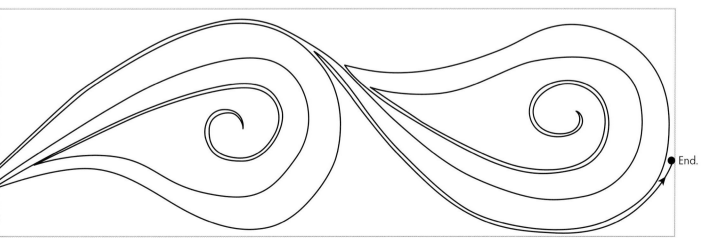

End.

Berried Feather

DESIGNED BY SHEILA SINCLAIR SNYDER

The feather is a versatile and timeless motif with endless possibilities for variation. To create this design, embellish a graceful feather by adding the extra touch of berries. The berries give the feather a different rhythm and size configuration. Use the method you prefer to sew them, either retracing or stitching them as figure eights. Sheila typically echoes the design (shown in blue) to give it more visibility on the quilt.

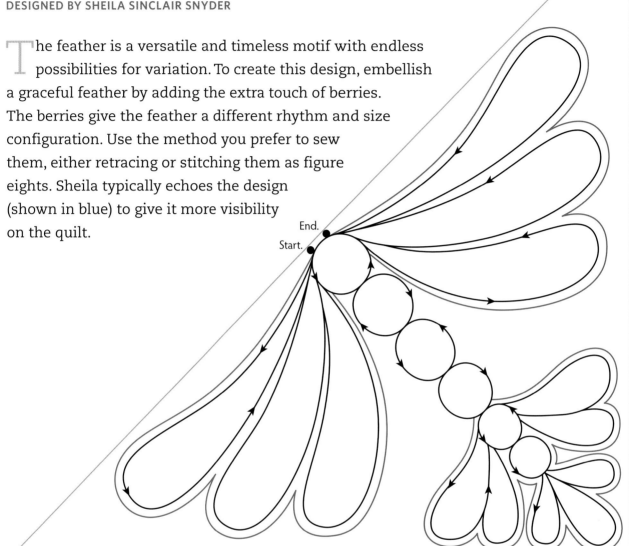

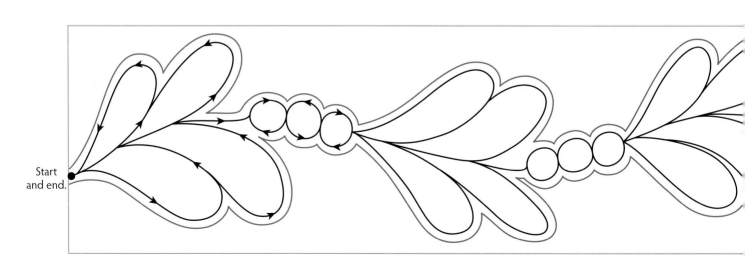

Start
and end.

About the Contributors

Karen M. Burns

Karen started with Martingale as an office-tour guide and then quickly worked her way into the heart of the company. As acquisitions editor, Karen has compiled many books and contributed to several more as a machine quilter.

Melissa Corry

HappyQuiltingMelissa.com

Melissa began quilting as a hobby in 2005 and started her blog in 2010. Her hobby has become a passion that she shares through tutorials, patterns, and her book *Irish Chain Quilts* (Martingale, 2015).

Lori Kennedy

TheInboxJaunt.com

Lori is a quilter, photographer, and blogger who specializes in free-motion quilting and modern whole-cloth quilting. Her blog series "Doodle Lessons" has become a hit with quilters and doodlers around the world.

Maddie Kertay

BadAssQuiltersSociety.com
SpoolQuilt.com

Maddie Kertay is a professional rabble-rouser and agent of change for the quilting world. Her ninja-like skills include free-motion long-arm quilting and quilt-store ownership.

April Rosenthal

AprilRosenthal.com

April is a fabric designer for Moda Fabrics, an author, and a quilter, homemaker, wife, and mama. She loves color, making things with her hands, learning, and the wind in the trees.

Vicki Ruebel

OrchidOwlQuilts.com

Vicki specializes in custom freehand quilting. Her award-winning quilts lean toward a contemporary aesthetic. She enjoys teaching and encouraging others to find their quilting voice.

Sheila Sinclair Snyder

LicensetoQuilt.com

Sheila is an award-winning quilter and teacher. She keeps her calendar full and interesting by traveling frequently to give lectures and teach workshops on long-arm quilting.

Angela Walters

QuiltingIsMyTherapy.com

Angela Walters is a long-arm quilter, teacher, fabric designer, and author. She has turned her love of stitches and fabric into a thriving business focused on modern machine quilting.

Christa Watson

ChristaQuilts.com

An award-winning sit-down machine quilter, Christa Watson designs quilt patterns, teaches workshops, and is the author of two machine-quilting books. Christa enjoys being a wife to her husband and a mom to her three kids.